Cover art by Christopher Lane cbl336@hotmail.com

Cover design by Todd Schafer todd@schaferdesign.net

Edited by Kristin Kearns kristin.kearns@gmail.com

ISBN: 978-1-304-84958-8

This book is dedicated to all young men and women on their transition into adulthood, whose choices will create the fabric of their lives.

It is also dedicated to those who strive for positive change in themselves and others, their community, and the world against the greatest of odds.

The Ocean Mafia

By Christopher Lane

Contents

The Ocean Mafia

By Christopher Lane

Preface

I grew up with a pack of surfers who achieved great heights and revolutionized modern surf culture. However, *The Ocean Mafia* is not based on any one person, or on any events that transpired in actuality. My imagination draws life from my experiences, and from teachings imparted to humanity from various spiritual sources. I wanted to take readers—especially young adults beginning their transition to adulthood—on a journey into the world of hard drug addiction, an exploration of unconditional love, redemption, gratitude, and service. At the heart of this story is the way in which our choices impact us and those around us. My hope is that readers will find within these pages inspiration for living a joyous life, attaining contentment through community, and accepting change and growing from life's challenges.

Chapter 1: The Heat of Transformation

With only one minute left in the final heat of the coveted five-star surfing competition, Jaime desperately needed a score of 9.5 out of 10 to be victorious. Only for a perfect wave, executed with seamless maneuvers, would the judges unanimously agree to give him the victory. Adding to his adrenaline rush was the fact that if he won this event, he would qualify for the Global Assault Surfing Tour, consisting of the best forty-two surfers in the world. As part of GAST, he would assuredly attract sponsors offering lucrative contracts and the chance to travel to exotic destinations, as well as surf some of the best waves on the planet. But Jaime wasn't in control of his fate: Mother Nature would decide if he was worthy. A perfect wave, delivered through her grace, had the power to change his reality in ways that he could never imagine.

Although the surf was well overhead, the ocean had gone flat like a lake, and he silently prayed to a higher power to send him a wave that would propel him into the surfing professionals' world tour. He'd started surfing at five years of age, when his father had taken him out tandem surfing on a soft-top longboard; a prodigy of the sport, Jaime was competing as a national team member by the time he was eight, and he had long dreamt of this climactic moment. He looked at his watch between paddle strokes, trying to stay close to his crosstown rival, Nate-dog, the one person besides Jaime who could change the outcome. At thirty seconds remaining he saw a wave break on an outer reef, signaling an approaching set, and although he had priority to take whatever wave he wanted over his competitor, if he chose the wrong one it could cost him the win.

Nate-dog had paddled inside him in a legal manner to catch the first wave of the set and was kicking his feet frantically, causing turbulence to keep Jaime from catching the wave. This turned out to be a blessing in disguise, as the second had the size and shape Jaime was looking for. Three, two, one: the high-pitched horn sounded, signaling the end of the heat, and Jaime caught the wave and stood up just in time for it to count; this was the moment of truth, his opportunity to take the reins of his destiny.

Jaime was in a timeless state, as like all great athletes he came into a zone: simply an attunement with the present moment. He free-fell off the vertical ledge, caught the rail of his surfboard, and bottom-turned into the gigantic barrel of blue-hued water. For precious moments he stayed inside the watery cavern, dragging his hand in the wave face to slow down his momentum, only to be spit out by the powerful compression of spray and into the light of day. He was still on the wave, an open canvas before him, and with a few sections to do turns that would add to his score. With lightning-quick speed and reflexes, Jaime floated over the first crumbly lip of whitewater as he and his board became one. This set him up to do a slashing maneuver under the lip, sending spray in a high-flying arc; he completed his barrage by busting a huge 360 aerial on the ramping end section into a flawless landing.

With an explosion of heart-released energy, he claimed the wave, arms in the air, his home crowd cheering, and looked to the cloudless blue sky. This was the moment he had visualized in his mind's eye before the heat; all of his training and preparation had paid off. But even though he was confident that he'd receive the scores he needed, it was up to the judges to affirm his vision.

He sat on his board near the shore break, and people ran into the water for autographs and pictures as he waited for the results to be posted. Jaime took a few full breaths and closed his eyes. When he opened them, the digital scoreboard had been updated. The international judges had awarded him perfect 10s, and the local crowd let loose with a thousand shouts of joy and congratulations. Nate had made it to the beach, wading in waist-deep water; he punched his board in anger, then put his hands over his face so that the spectators wouldn't see his cries of frustration. In direct contrast, Jaime was ecstatic. This contest was being held at the point break he'd grown up on, and as he arrived at the beach, his closest friends, Robbie and Sage, lifted him onto their shoulders and carried him to the podium. Jaime raised his fists and screamed to the heavens; never had he been so overwhelmed by emotion. This was a day that he would remember forever, and the happiest moment of his young life.

As the awards commentator lifted Jaime's arm, making it official, and presented him with his trophy, a bitter Nate-dog sprayed him with a much-shaken-up bottle of champagne. Jaime, basking in the glory, swallowed as much of the bubbly brew as he could and spat a hydrant of it back in Nate's face. The crowd erupted in laughter as a scowling Nate walked off the podium, cursing Jaime under his breath and vowing to get his revenge. The trophy, a bronze-plated wave, bore the names of past champions, with *Bullet-Head Point 5-Star* inscribed on its wooden base. Lifting it over his head, Jaime gave thanks to his local sponsors and those who had supported him in his rise to the top, and promised he'd make them proud. The fact that the contest was in his native city added to the experience; it had been a grueling year of traveling to get the points needed to qualify and validation as a world-class competitor. He'd competed in every major event, against the best surfers from every nation, all vying for the top sixteen slots that would catapult them into the GAST circuit. This contest gave him enough points to squeeze into that elite group.

After he'd received his first-place check and talked to the media, he snuck through the competitors' area, out the back door and away from the masses, down one of the side streets he'd grown up on. Jaime wasn't comfortable around so many people. He wanted to celebrate with his girlfriend, who had watched the contest on television back at his pad, too anxious to view it from the cliff. Many of the houses he passed were unkempt, with overgrown foliage serving as property boundaries, though others were colorfully decorated and landscaped in unique and artistic ways. Surf-related gear appeared in odd places throughout the neighborhood: booties tied together and hung from power lines; old, damaged surfboards repurposed as fences and as walls for the paint-splattered tree forts that the kids used in their war games.

Still in his wetsuit to stay warm in the brisk ocean breeze, surfboard under his arm and trophy in his backpack, Jaime jogged past the house where the boys had shoved his head down the toilet and repeatedly flushed it to prepare him for tube riding. They had also hung him upside-down off the redwood tree for countless minutes, to simulate being suspended in air during a wipeout—one of the many initiations for a young surfer in this backwoods neighborhood. Every dwelling held a host of memories that flashed through his mind like a life review. Jaime remembered vividly the rundown drug house where, when he was thirteen, the Bullet-Head boys made him take his first bong hit of marijuana as an initiation into their ranks, but only after forcing him to eat a jar of pickled pigs' feet, which he later vomited for hours in a stoned stupor. Jaime knew now, as he passed these dwellings, that no longer would he be a punching bag for his peers; he had entered a new phase of his life and would leave these ghosts in the past.

He considered himself lucky to have experienced so much at a young age, but, running toward his girlfriend's arms, he knew with all certainty that this was just the beginning: he was embarking on a new chapter of his life. A group of the local boys was partying at Cement Beach, an abandoned lot where inebriated sunbathers lazed on lounge chairs and disintegrating couches with forty-ouncers in hand, screaming obscenities at all who passed. Hip-hop music blared from a sticker-laden boom box. Most if not all of the Cement Beach crew didn't surf, although they dressed the part, in clothing and hats emblazoned with popular surf logos, and critiqued others for their shortcomings in the water. Nobody escaped their narrow-minded discrimination; too inebriated to form a sentence, they generally issued their slander as one- or two-word attacks. Conversations were usually centered on negative subjects: who got in a fight with whom, how wasted they had been, and the classic complaints of how much this town sucked and how many outsiders were infiltrating their territory.

They yelled at Jaime to join in the festivities, and berated him when he didn't stop: sarcastic cries of "Oh, too cool" and "Go run home to mommy!" Through surfing countless hours every day and practicing mixed martial arts, Jaime had turned his tall and lanky body into a finely tuned instrument, and the Cement Beach crew knew to only verbally challenge him. He understood that this was their way of trying to feel better about themselves, as they watched someone else break out of the pack and achieve great heights as a pro surfer.

Neighbors and family friends came out of their homes, shouted his name and waved. He enjoyed the recognition, hard-earned as it had been through a dysfunctional family life and growing up in the sharp-edged surfing subculture. Now he knew he was destined for fame. He had been granted an opportunity to change the course of his life, although he was unaware of the trials and tribulations he would face on his heroic journey.

Chapter 2: Legends Arise and Fall

Walking triumphantly through the tropically landscaped side yard of the house he'd grown up in, Jaime heard his father yelling at his mother, and the shattering of glass. He knew these sounds all too well, and knew that it was best to sneak around the house to his private hut in the backyard. His father was an alcoholic, and although he wasn't physically abusive, he spat out vicious words of criticism at Jaime for trying to be a competitive surfer, and verbally abused Jaime's mother during his frequent drunken binges. A past longboard legend, known for his effortless style and ability to hang all ten toes over the nose of his surfboard while riding a wave, he had destroyed his life through alcoholism, and when he got drunk he would go on rampages about the politics of the sport and how wave riding had become an ego-driven pursuit. In Jaime's dad's time, competitive surfing wasn't yet accepted, and the culture had more of a soul-surfer philosophy: share the ocean and have fun. Contests and surfing magazines were seen as the commercialization of an activity that was more in tune with nature than with the ego of man.

Jaime thought otherwise. He enjoyed the competitive aspect of the sport as well as the oneness with nature he felt while in the ocean. In this era, unlike his father's, surfers were paid well, and there were plenty of sponsors that would fund his way around the world, not only for his revered freestyle surfing but also for his competitive prowess. What better opportunity to explore life and travel while he was young and free? From his youthful perspective, competition had expanded the horizons of surfing on every level, and he had a passion to reach greatness through doing the thing he loved the most. He was moving into a new phase of his life as an adult; experience had not yet shown him that those who embark on the path of greatness will undoubtedly encounter merciless challenges, which can make them change direction and retreat from their good intentions. And without proper role models and family support, one can lose their way amidst the obstacles to their ambitions. Being a successful pro surfer is a difficult task, and only a select few can earn a good living from it. One must have the foresight and guidance to create a backup plan in case of injury or incompetence as one of thousands of frothing athletes vying for the top spots.

In any event, Jaime would soon be moving in with his girlfriend, Ivette, to get away from his father's madness, but with conflicting feelings: he wanted to be there for his mother, whom he loved dearly and who had endured much suffering from his father's cruel ways. She was the most positive influence in Jaime's life. She'd raised him to be polite and respectful of all things great and small, all people regardless of class or culture, and she had planted seeds in his psyche that had yet to blossom. From the universal truths and wisdom of the ages she had whispered in his ear as a toddler, to the infinite love and guidance she had showered upon him throughout his life, she was the main reason he stood in the hallway of recognition for his talents, which he had worked hard to cultivate outside of her nest, in an environment where most dreamers were met with scorn.

Jaime also had fond memories of spending time with his father as a child: sitting perched on his shoulders watching the waves; surfing together for hours, his father pushing Jaime, not strong enough to paddle on his own, into the breakers. He remembered vividly the feeling of his father's strong arm guiding him on the surfboard, like a missile into the liquid landscape—as if he were on a magic carpet sailing through the universe. It wasn't until his late adolescence that his father's alcohol issues took over, and changed their relationship in a drastic way. Jaime was a product of his mother and his father, two contrasting sides that would set his future in motion.

He opened the door to his self-contained surf shack, and Ivette greeted him with a big hug and a kiss. She had picked jasmine and lavender from his mother's garden and hung them from a string above the window. The flowers made the space smell sweet and sexy, just like her.

"Congratulations, honey, you did it! You made the tour!"

"I know!" Jaime reveled in what now seemed a dream. "I can't believe it really happened."

"You were right; your strategy of waiting for the best waves paid off," Ivette said. She and Jaime had known each other since preschool, when they played carefree in the soft, warm sand, forming a lasting bond. He had asked Ivette to the high school prom, where his teenage hormones had reached a boiling point, and they had been in a relationship ever since. She was the first love of his life, and he could see a future with her. Her long blond locks fell over both of their shoulders, and her piercing green eyes looked into his soul. They jumped up and down in synchronicity, as if on a trampoline composed of stars and planets. Jaime had never felt so happy and accomplished, and in love with Ivette.

Unexpectedly, his door was kicked open with a wood-shattering smash against the wall. His father stood in the doorway, drunk and with bloodshot eyes, a bottle of whisky in his swollen hand and a look of incoherence on his sun-damaged face. "You think you're something now," he slurred. "You aren't nothing but a little piece of shit who needs to be flushed down the toilet. I thought I told you surfing contests were for morons!"

It was the first time he'd invaded Jaime's shack. Until now, Jaime had managed to shield Ivette from his father's sickness, and he was embarrassed for her to see him this way. He had never talked back to his father, for fear of a physical confrontation, and he wasn't about to start. He grabbed Ivette's hand and they ran past his father, who was now on his knees, crying and mumbling obscenities. Jaime felt bad, but he knew he couldn't help, and he had to get away from this toxic environment.

He crashed at Ivette's that night. She lived a few blocks away, in a safe, forest-like setting, in a cottage surrounded by towering oak trees. They lay together in her cushiony bed, listening to the surf crash on the shore in the distance. Jaime wondered aloud why his father couldn't control the disease that was ruining his life, and whether there was some form of truth in his condemnation of competitive surfing. Ivette ran her hands through his hair, comforting him like a warm blanket, even though she couldn't fully comprehend the inner demons that tormented him.

In the morning he returned to his parents' house, to retrieve his belongings and say goodbye to his mom. Before going in, he looked through the stained-glass front window, its rainbow of colors faded with time. His father had passed out on the couch, and his mother was wiping his forehead with a towel. She looked like a glowing angel of light, with her white dress and long, snow-white hair. And she was; she had always taken care of both of them and never cast judgment for their actions. She was the rock, the foundation that kept their family together, and Jaime would do anything for the sake of her well-being.

He entered through the creaky screen door he'd walked through innumerable times, into the living room, where marks on the doorjamb tracked his stages of growth, and framed photos and magazine pictorials illustrating his surfing prowess adorned the walls. His mother turned to him, her timeless features relaxed, eyes penetrating. Their gazes met in silence. No words needed to be said, no love needed to be proclaimed, for it was broadcast from her heart in a way that speech couldn't communicate. She had known this time would come, and was ready to give him the freedom he needed. But not before she said, "Follow your heart, my son, and you will never be led astray. Someone is watching over you and will be guiding you toward goodness always."

"No words can express how grateful I am to you for showing me the path to my dreams. I will always be here for you, as you have been for me," Jaime said, in a poetic language unlike the surf slang he used with his friends. He loved that his mother stayed positive and uplifting regardless of external circumstances. Throughout his youth she had driven him up and down the coast to surfing competitions, and coached him with her motherly presence. Knowing that he was never alone, that she was on the beach watching and rooting him on, made him surf his best. His competitive struggles had centered around staying focused and continuing to improve, and learning to be indifferent to the results. She had taught him that as long as he had given it his best, he should have no regrets, and to always be thankful for the wondrous life he was living.

"Jaime, my son, I have something to give you. Your father and I have saved it for this day." She went into her bedroom and emerged with a silver necklace, its pendant depicting a dolphin in a jumping silhouette. She knew Jaime loved dolphins. "Dogs of the sea," as he described them: always playful, the ocean dweller's best friend for the way they protected humans from sharks and swam side by side with surfers on a wave. The necklace was meant as a talisman, to protect Jaime as he gained his independence.

He hugged her goodbye and said that he would be back soon. It was time for him to journey into the life lessons that lay before him. This would be his initiation into the real world, a rite all men and women go through once they leave their parents' house. He picked up his board bag, into which he had crammed all his belongings, and stepped out the door, off the lit path of his mother's guidance and into an ocean of possibilities.

Chapter 3: Wake-Up Call

Jaime awoke early, Ivette sound asleep by his side. It took the call of the waves to break him away from her warm body. He smiled at the morning sunlight beaming through the majestic trees just outside. Without showering or looking in the mirror, oblivious to the mohawk his short, blond hair had formed as he slept, he put on his jeans, a hoodie, and sandals. The first contest of the season was coming up in February, three months away. Now that he'd qualified for GAST, all he had to do was concentrate on his surfing prowess and prepare; but his psyche hadn't fully absorbed this benediction, or what he'd have to do—and give up—to succeed as a world-class professional surfer. After making a rich cup of coffee to get psyched for his surf session, he grabbed his skateboard and left Ivette's house. The skateboard's big, soft wheels were forgiving over the small rocks and displaced pavement, and Jaime did slalom turns down the street to the ocean, cup of joe in hand, mimicking riding an imaginary wave while practicing surfing-related body mechanics. With a skidding 180-degree turn, and without spilling a drop of his dark brew, he skated up to the metal rail that separated the street from the rugged coastline.

Glassy waves peeled into the seemingly endless bay; no one was out, a rare occurrence except for at the crack of dawn, when it was too cold to surf and great white sharks hunted their prey. Jaime sat down on the smooth wooden bench that had been there for as long as he could remember, names of locals and graffiti underneath the layers of resin used to preserve this artifact of cultural history, and surveyed the coastline from north to south. He wondered how other spots might be, given this westerly swell, and thought about what size and model surfboard he'd ride given the current conditions. The swell was on the rise, and tomorrow, if it kept building as forecasted, he planned to surf Nightmares, one of the premier big wave spots in the world, with Robbie and Sage.

The town was divided into two sections, as far as the surfers' boundaries were concerned. Each side of town—north and south—had its local rights to certain surf spots, although some on the unwritten borders were shared. Bullet-Head Point was the heart of Jaime's surf zone on the south side, and the main peak at the tip of the Point, Bullets, was ruled by shaved-headed locals. You didn't want to paddle out there unless you were one of the boys or knew someone, and infiltrating the pack was something few outsiders could ever aspire to do. Bullets was a fast, right-hand reef break, with three distinct sections that linked together when the waves were big. Bullet-Head Point was so named because of the self-proclaimed "Bullet-Head boys," who, trained in jiujitsu and mixed martial arts, listened to hardcore punk rock and surfed with an aggressive flair. Heavily tattooed and antagonistic toward strangers, they governed the lineup and regulated the ocean in their backyard.

There had been a changing of the guard back when the longboard generation ended and the shortboard era began. The surfing culture changed drastically during this transition, from soul-surfer camaraderie and relaxed wave riding to the "destroy and attack" generation that wanted to maximize every section of the wave to the beach with flair and aplomb, and claim it. The Bullet-Head boys were the sons of the longboard legends, and had been passed the baton of the ocean mafia: those who controlled the surfing zone that was their territory, and would enforce strict codes of conduct for anyone who wasn't in their circle. One's place in the pecking order was determined based on talent and local status, and it was every surfer for himself once positioned in the lineup.

Jaime didn't consider himself a Bullet-Head, and refused to shave his head so as to maintain his own identity, but he was one of them whether he liked it or not, born into a surfing family that spanned three generations. His late grandfather had surfed, but he'd taken it up as a recreational activity later in his life, after relocating to the area from the East Coast. Like most grommets, the local term for young surfers, Jaime had been tortured, beaten, and abused in a variety of sick and sadistic ways by his peers. His punishers had been raised to believe that it was the tough love you received that would prepare you for the harsh, unpredictable conditions of the ocean, and trying to rebel against these beatings would only make it worse. Still other elders, commonly known as "carps" in the community, would take out their personal problems or power trips on the younger crew, unleashing unprovoked verbal and physical attacks that ranged from mild beat-downs to life-threatening hazing ceremonies. It was this unhealthy environment of abuse that led to low self-esteem and drug addiction. On Bullet-Head Point, only the strong survived.

Jaime felt like a black sheep at times, and had high aspirations to see more of the world. He'd traveled outside the country many times for contests, but always under his coaches' and mom's supervision, and he hadn't had the chance to explore beyond the surfing arena. There seemed to be so much more in life than these four walls of disharmony, other ways of existing than that of the surf ghetto he'd been born into. Now his dreams seemed poised to come true. He took a deep breath as he lounged on the bench, looking out into the horizon, and sighed with a contentment he hadn't felt in a long time, if ever.

Down the street Jaime could see the boys pulling up to the parking zone: a dirt lot on the edge of the cliff, each spot reserved for one of the local crew. In place of "No Parking" signs, comical graffiti showed scenes of what happened to outsiders both in and out of the water, and the boys shot harsh looks if you dared to enter their space. Out-of-towners who made the mistake of parking in one of their spots would quite often have their windows waxed and tires deflated.

Although he had a kinship with this pack of surfers, Jaime felt that the local surfing culture had degenerated into needless violence, drugs, and unwarranted discrimination against misperceived alien invaders of their home breaks. The area had been a drug haven since its inception, and it was now overpopulated because of the quality surf breaks that attracted surfers from all over the planet. Jaime was a humble, quiet person. When he had a problem with someone while surfing, he tried to be as nice as possible, even when the other surfer's inexperience had put him in a life-threatening situation, and politely explain the rules and etiquette of the sport. He had learned through his martial arts training that it never feels good to be angry. In fact, anger wastes energy, even if it feels justified, and Jaime prided himself on retaining his center in order to deal calmly with life's difficulties. In any event, one of the Bullet-Heads would always do the dirty work, which usually involved dunkings underwater, and being told to go in and never come back.

Jaime had watched as too many surfers with vast potential had destroyed their lives through alcoholism and addiction. He knew that being a surfer was a great gift, a gift that could be taken away at any moment, and he tried to live his life in a way that was a reflection of this concept. This meant being grateful, enjoying every moment as much as possible, and being kind to others. His loving mother had taught him these secrets to living a happy life; the kinder you were to others, the more doors would be opened, and people would help you in myriad ways. This mind-set of kindness and compassion was considered a weakness in this town, and went against the grain of the collective. From a young age Jaime had known that he was different, and he had kept his view of life secret, along with his desire to move on from the cage of negativity that trapped him.

"Yeah, Jaime-boy!" Robbie shouted out the passenger window of Sage's massive truck, which they'd nicknamed the Black Beast. It had limo-tinted windows, a four-inch lift kit with oversized tires, and a camper shell that made it look more like a tank than a four-by-four. Sage and Robbie both looked the military part, with shaved heads and chiseled features, except Robbie was tall and lean, while Sage was a short, thick-necked bulldog type. Both had a multitude of tattoos and wore ribbed black tank tops, traditional Bullet-Head Point garb. Sage parked alongside the rail, so other cars would have to go around his truck on the narrow ocean boulevard, and he and Robbie jumped out and gave Jaime powerful high-fives. They congratulated him on his win and recounted, with hand movements and sound effects, the last-second wave that won him the contest and a spot on the tour. Jaime had grown up with these guys, and, unlike the others, they were like real brothers to him; years ago they had taken a blood oath, slicing their index fingers and taping them together, to watch out for each other under all circumstances. They had all come from dysfunctional family environments and bonded as adolescents, but they'd turned out fairly level-headed from having to take care of themselves from a young age.

Without a second thought, Robbie opened his hand to reveal a glistening, lime-green bud. He gave it a slight squeeze, placed it under Jaime's nose so he could get a whiff, and proceeded to roll a gigantic, sweet-smelling blunt to celebrate the victory. There was a place underneath the cliff where everyone hung out and watched the waves, and they jumped over the rail and walked down the rocky goat trail to get high. Nearly all of the locals smoked cannabis, pure herb or mixed with tobacco, whether they surfed or not; it was a big part of the local economy and considered a sacred plant, with a multitude of uses as a medicine. Everyone knew Bullet-Head Point was the place to score the best ganja, and the boys were the main players in the game.

"Yeah, you sizzled Nate-dog so hard, Jaime, that was sick!" Sage let out between lung-bursting coughs, and he passed the rich joint of marijuana rolled in a tobacco leaf. Nate was Jaime's competitive rival from the north side, and although they got along decently on land, they were bitter enemies in the ocean, having surfed heats against each other since they were grommets on the junior-pro circuit.

"Hey, Jaime, the boys are throwing a party for you tonight at Vinnie's house," Sage said, with post-toke excitement. Vinnie was the old-school legend of Bullet-Head Point, from long before it was given its name, so not only did Jaime want to go, he would be honored to attend. Vinnie was Native American and looked it, with his straight, long, black hair, his intense amber eyes and olive skin. His family dated back to a time when this was Indigenous land, although he was the last of his people in the area. He was like an uncle to the boys, and his house was a refuge from the storms of life—his door always open to those in need, whether on drugs or sober. He was also the Point's leading tattoo artist, and while poking his ink gun into their skin, he'd recount to the boys the history and legacy of the area, and give warnings about the curse left for those who desecrated this sacred ground. According to Vinnie, you would be haunted by evil spirits as long as you lived on this burial site of his ancestors, and you would search for happiness but never find it.

For the boys and Jaime, it was more like a campfire storytelling session than real fact, but they had respect for

Vinnie and would listen intently to his fables as the pain from the needles took them to the place he described. Numerous drug houses littered the neighborhood, and you could get whatever type of drug you wanted from one of the many vendors. It was a place where kids shouldn't be raised, and you needed to put bars on your windows to protect yourself from the bold and desperate thieves. At night they would come out like the junkie apocalypse, rummaging through trash cans and breaking into cars, anything they could sell for their next high. Surely this was the hellish existence Vinnie's forefathers had prophesized, but the boys didn't yet have the wisdom or experience to see that their fate, and the lives they were living, was what he spoke of.

Later that night the party was going off, with Jaime's friends and all of the locals in attendance. Vinnie's was the place where everyone from the neighborhood hung out and played common games like cards, ping-pong, pool, and horseshoes. On any given day people came and went, some to pass time or receive tattoos, others to have a few beers with whomever was willing. This night was like many others; there was always a reason to celebrate, especially when one of their own had achieved success as a professional surfer.

Although Jaime was mild-mannered and polite, he had a dark side, and he drank alcohol and dabbled in other recreational drugs. He also had a susceptibility to addiction, since his father was an alcoholic and many of his friends were addicted to some type of drug or drink. Born and raised in such an environment, he had grown up with a pack of alpha males bred from the same causation. Luckily for Jaime, his mother had set him straight as a teenager by showing up at parties when he was wasted, pulling his ear and taking him home, embarrassing him in front of everyone. Then she'd lecture him on the consequences of going down the same road as his father and countless others.

Now, of legal age and on his own, Jaime was free to do whatever he wanted. He felt he could control his impulses and use pot and alcohol in moderation, keeping hard drugs for special occasions. Currently, his only addictions were weed and caffeine, which he considered harmless and part of his daily routine. But tonight he was ready to have a good time.

Shortly after his arrival at the party, the onslaught of debauchery began, and in his haste, Jaime forgot his plans for the next day. Before he knew it, he was taking obligatory shots of tequila and having a beer bong stuck down his throat. Sticky joints were being passed around like little torches in the night, and to the hypnotic beat of his favorite hip-hop artists they danced the night away, blurred bodies bouncing against each other like bumper cars in an amusement park. Ivette was somewhere, but Jaime, on the verge of blacking out and in a pickled state of mind, had lost sight of her hours ago. Other local girls were grinding up against him, and he couldn't help but run his hands over their tight bodies and receive wet kisses on the cheeks and lips.

Sometime past midnight Jaime found himself in an unbreakable headlock, being dragged into the back bedroom by an unknown assailant. Trying to focus on the people surrounding him, he realized it was some of the Bullet-Head boys. They were laughing hysterically, like a frenzy of hyenas that had found their prey. "C'mon, Jaime-boy, try some of this," they urged.

Jaime saw the white substance on the table and knew what it was, and in his drunkenness he figured, Why not? He took the rolled-up dollar bill and snorted a long line of little white crystals. It was an innocent act that would have dire consequences: as if someone had given him a shot of adrenaline, Jaime's pupils dilated, and he felt a surge of energy up his spine. No longer drunk, but fired up on cocaine, he chatted with the boys about a bond they shared, which didn't really exist, and they snorted line after line into the early hours of the morning. At one point, Jaime's jaw frantically moving from side to side as he waited for his next bump, Ivette peeked into the room.

"Ivette, where'd you go? I—I—was waiting for you to come . . ." But before he could finish his garbled, parrot-tongued sentence she was gone. He couldn't have cared less in the state he was in. He had never felt more energetic and God-like . . . until the high after each line became shorter and shorter, and the cravings became deeper and deeper, and he sank into a self-created well of craving he couldn't climb out of.

The orange morning sun was now rising, and people were going home, leaving Jaime shivering on the couch, craving another line to keep the good feeling alive. He had no idea how much drugs he had done, and felt like he was going to die. With short gasps of air and cold sweat soaking his body, he passed out for a few hours, but awoke with a sickening fear, remembering that today was the day he was supposed to surf the biggest and most dangerous wave on earth—Nightmares.

Chapter 4: Nightmares

He didn't feel up for it, still quivering from the past night's alcohol and drug abuse, his mind in a haze and his energy nonexistent. But today was the day, and the swell that they had been tracking and waiting for, the first big one of the season, was showing fifteen feet every twenty seconds—huge by any standard. Its northwest direction was perfect for Nightmares, which was thus far undiscovered by the masses, a private proving ground for the world's elite big wave riders. To brave the bitter cold water you needed a thick, hooded wetsuit, with booties for your feet and gloves for your hands, or in a few minutes they would lose all sensation and turn into frozen stumps. With its combination of ice-cold, shark-infested waters and a takeoff zone that was beyond vertical, Nightmares was the heaviest big wave break without comparison. Every drop into the wave was a trial of your skills; and your sentence, if you didn't make it, was to be swept into the shallow, boulder-laden reef and devoured by the mouth of the barrel, or possibly thrown into the rocky pillars that jutted out of the ocean floor. Jaime knew this was going to be a life or death situation, although he had no premonition of the tragic unfolding of the day's events.

Robbie and Sage picked Jaime up in the Black Beast, honking the horn and revving the engine as he quietly gathered his surf gear from Ivette's storage shed, and they roared up the coast well before sunrise. They had also partied all night and were still wired on meth, a drug that had wiped out many lives in the community. Their usage was moderate, but meth was becoming their drug of choice, as the addictive tentacles wrapped around their reasoning and mental faculties. The drug's aftermath kept you on edge for hours, if not days, and although Robbie and Sage were in high spirits, it was a pseudo-good feeling that in time would rob you of your life force. Sage had meticulously rolled a perfect joint with a paper crutch, and they puffed and coughed in a pre-surf ritual that soothed their nerves and overactive minds.

"What happened last night?" Jaime asked sarcastically, and rolled his eyes as Robbie and Sage chuckled in recollection.

"What, you don't remember having a threesome with those two hotties?" joked Sage, gently jabbing him in the arm.

"Yeah, I guess I went a little overboard," Jaime said, though he did not yet know the extent of the damage he had done.

Robbie had prepared strong coffee, and the truck's cab pulsated to the music's beat as they fueled up, sharing from the stainless-steel thermos lid. After a thirty-minute drive past rolling hills and fresh, green fields dotted with cows, they turned down a private farm road, accessible through a locked gate to which only landowners and registered guests had the code. Anyone caught sneaking in would be banned forever, and quite possibly taken out to the woods, stripped naked, and left to fend for themselves. Over the years they'd seen more than a few men jogging in the nude along the freeway with shriveled bits, eyes trained straight ahead in humiliation as they made their way back into town. It was a hilarious sight, and the boys would heckle out the window and try to find a puddle to spray the jogger as they drove by. Rarely, if ever, was the trespasser one of their local contingent of big wave brethren.

It was foggy that morning, but the sun was rising in the gray mist behind them as they checked the ocean conditions. They parked overlooking the breakers and suited up in the frigid air, teeth chattering to the heavy metal blaring from the truck's powerful stereo system. Their wetsuits were dry and toasty, and once they put them on, they felt more at ease in their second skin.

They heard a loud rustling in the bushes, and one of the locals emerged in a cloud of dust. The boys had nicknamed him Rags because he came from a wealthy family but had ended up a homeless drug addict. A promising surfer in his youth, Rags now wandered the coastline, appearing in the most unusual of places. His skin had turned brown from uncleanliness, and his matted hair was naturally turning into dreadlocks, giving him the appearance of a Rastafarian. Besides the ragged clothing that he wore, his only other possession was his long bamboo drum, which he beat on when surfers entered the ocean at Nightmares.

"Hey guys, you got a few bucks I can borrow, or some chronic smoke?" He grinned, revealing missing and rotting teeth.

"Yeah, no problem, Rags. Here's a couple bucks and a bud," Sage offered.

They felt sorry for Rags, and would help him out when they could, but they had grown up around many addicts, so his misfortune didn't faze them too much. They were more focused on the task at hand. Despite the comfort provided by their neoprene superman suits, a subtle anxiety coursed through their minds, though they wouldn't speak of it to each other. They had all surfed Nightmares on smaller days, but the size of today's waves was what would give Jaime the experience he needed: he had to prove to himself, and his peers, that he could ride surf of this size if he was to gain respect as an elite big wave rider.

It was an easy paddle out. Jumping off the headland and paddling into the bay, you would find yourself in the takeoff spot in a few minutes. Since the bay was a marine sanctuary, no watercraft were allowed, which meant it was a paddle-only wave. And when it got too big, no matter what size board you rode, chances were that paddling into the wave would be impossible. Today no one else wanted a piece of its ferocity, and they had it all to themselves, aside from the barking packs of mammoth seals and other ocean inhabitants, and Rags methodically beating on his drum at the tip of the point, as they jumped off the cliff and into their fate.

Jaime, Sage, and Robbie sat outside of where the waves broke, a hundred yards before the mountains of water poured from a deep trench to break upon the boulder-strewn reef. “You ready for this, Jaime-boy?” Sage grabbed him by the shoulder and shook him a little bit to ring his bell. In fact his bell had been rung the night before, and it was still ringing in his head.

“Yeah, let’s do this, brotha.” Jaime forced an air of confidence, but he had never been so scared in his life. He felt like he was going to vomit, and he took some calming breaths and tried to put on his game face. A sound erupted, like the rumble of an earthquake, as the set that had passed underneath them, lifting them like buoys high in the air, crashed into the bay. Rags started beating his drum louder and faster, to signal the oncoming set that they had yet to see. There was no lifeguard or water patrol, no hospital close by or anyone to help them should things go wrong; the boys were on their own, with only their waterman’s skills to depend on.

They looked at each other one last time, recognizing that this was an unparalleled moment in their many surf sessions together. Then they paddled into the takeoff zone and waited. They had timed the sets at five-minute intervals, so they thought that they had a few minutes to ready themselves for the possible ride of their lives. Hearts beating rapidly, they saw the approaching set a mile out to sea. It was as if a dark veil were rising before them, slowly rolling closer, pulling all into its vortex. They knew not to take the first wave of the set, as it would suck all the water off the reef, and if you didn't make the drop or fell, you might be thrown onto the rock bed or held underwater for multiple waves.

They paddled for their lives over a succession of four-story waves, each bigger than the last. Nothing could have prepared Jaime for this, and feeling depleted didn't help. Robbie, with his long and muscular arms, was a stronger paddler and had extra energy from his meth high, and he was now twenty yards ahead. He turned around easily, paddling into one of the larger waves of the set. As Jaime paddled over the shoulder, he saw his soul brother bottom-turn into the carnivorous pit.

As if in tunnel vision, the wave Jaime would take came into focus. He whipped in the opposite direction his ten-foot-two gun and stroked into the seaborne monster beneath him. Blinding offshore winds held him up in the lip; it was too late to pull back, and he jumped to his feet and into by far the biggest wave of his life.

He fell with a shimmering chandelier of liquid diamonds, suspended in space, until the impact. Somehow his board was underneath his feet as he landed mid-face, but still in a precarious position as the gigantic shadow of the wave darkened the waterscape around him. Instinctively he became one with his board, as he bottom-turned into the throat of nature. Thirty feet or more above him a waterfall shot over his head, creating a tunnel of seawater by opposing forces; to be in the belly of something like this was incomparable to anything in life. All who have experienced riding inside a giant wave will say the same: no words can describe the feeling of bliss and oneness that comes from that act. Jaime could hear his labored breath as he navigated toward the cavernous exit of light.

The inner compression of the huge barrel made a cannon-like explosion of spray, which spat Jaime out of its core and into daylight. He was going the speed of light, his surfboard making a high-pitched hum in tune with the sound of the wind blowing up the wave face. There was no turning or attempting maneuvers on this erect wall of water; he was racing toward the channel, where he would contend with the last section of the wave.

Things seemed to go into slow motion. A glacier-sized chunk of water landed on his head, crushing him with the force of a hundred trash compactors into the dark depths of the sea. With the wind knocked out of his lungs and barely conscious, Jaime felt that he was watching his lifeless body suspended in a watery casket. In this altered dimension, he saw a pod of dolphins come to his aid, pushing him upward. Then, abruptly, his eyes opened wide, and he was filled with energy as his body's lifesaving protocol went into effect. He was in complete darkness, aware only of the grating sound of massive boulders on the sea floor. He didn't know which way was up or down, but as he swam into the light, the current pulled him to the safety zone.

He surfaced, coughing water in the thick foam and gasping for air, only to see another titanic wave about to break on top of his head. Down he went again, this time smashed into unconsciousness and sent spiraling through a kaleidoscopic tunnel. Time stopped as his life flashed before him, a review of the effect that he had on himself and others, all of his life events coexisting in a three-dimensional sphere around him. A portal materialized that he was drawn to, when out of the ether and nearly unbearable to view, a being of light appeared before him, telling him it wasn't his time—that he had to go back, that he had more to do in this life's incarnation. He was in the omnipotent presence of a heavenly being, and his spirit rebelled against his return to the material world after feeling as if he had returned home from a long journey. The next thing Jaime knew, he woke up to the sight of his mother sleeping in the corner of his hospital room, and the feeling of being encased in a damaged and bruised body. He wept, not so much at the physical pain, but for what he had seen and felt, and the knowledge that he couldn't return to that indescribable place of pure love, that he had always longed for in his heart.

Chapter 5: The Downward Spiral

The rogue wave that had broken in the channel had knocked Jaime unconscious, and he would have surely drowned had it not been for the quick thinking of Robbie. He had seen it all, and risked his life by paddling into the impact zone, taking off his leash, and diving into the depths of the sea. With strength he didn't know he had, and his meth high kicking into overdrive, Robbie swam like a triathlete to Jaime's aid; if Jaime was going to drown, he would die trying to save him.

Jaime's motionless body floated like a rag doll underwater. Robbie grabbed him around the waist and swam to the surface. They appeared a mere twenty yards from the wall of rocky outcropping and pillars of reef, but just when Robbie was sure that they were doomed, a backwash of whitewater pushed them away from danger. Sage had just ridden his mammoth wave with success, and was abuzz with joy, when he saw the boys floating in the bay, Robbie waving his arms frantically. Jaime was still out cold, but breathing. Robbie had abandoned his surfboard and Jaime's had been bashed to pieces on the cliff after his wipeout, so they paddled him on Sage's board to the beach.

After an agonizing ten minutes, they arrived at the shore pound, where they saw that they had to contend with large, unruly and shifting riptides.

They took Jaime off Sage's board so that they could both hold him as they navigated the swim to the beach. At this point they didn't know whether he was alive or dead, but they put his limp arms over their shoulders, each with one arm around his midsection, and swam as one. Whether because of luck or divine intervention, a wave broke behind them as they battled the rip current, and it propelled them forward in the whitewater, far enough that they could dig their feet in the sand. Once out of danger they laid Jaime on the beach, and Sage ran like a jaguar back along the cliff to retrieve the Black Beast. On the drive to the hospital Robbie sat in the back of the truck with Jaime's head on his lap, telling him he was going to be all right and praying he would make it.

When Jaime awoke, head pulsing and pain coursing through his entire body, his mother was there to greet him, and she assumed his tears were from the shock of the accident. Though he had grown up among a wild pack of surfers, it was his mother who had taught him the most important things in life, and he had always felt her unconditional love for him; it eased his intense pain and comforted him to have her there, and her presence helped him to transition back into his body after his near-death experience. He had been unconscious for two days, and in her soft-spoken way, she informed him that he had broken his lower leg, sprained his back and neck, and had a serious concussion. It could have been much worse, and he was lucky to be alive, thanks to Robbie and Sage's Herculean effort to save him.

The first question that came to his mind was whether he would be healed within three months, in time to surf in the first GAST contest of the competitive season. When the doctor stopped in, Jaime got his answer: in a dry, matter-of-fact tone, the doctor projected a three- to six-month healing time frame for his leg and a year of rehabilitation. This estimate was general, said the doctor, and didn't take into consideration the individual's drive to get better. It also didn't account for other factors, such as what the patient put into his or her body, which could drastically alter one's recovery. But in his shell-shocked frame of mind, Jaime felt that he had been given a death sentence.

Having never faced this type of adversity, it was like being told his life was over; everything he had worked for had been taken away from him without warning. For a professional surfer and finely trained athlete, the prospect of sitting out of the water was sheer torture, especially when he could have been surfing tropical waves in a distant land on the GAST world tour with only a few guys out. Jaime thought back to how he had gotten wasted the night before, and wondered if things would have been different if he'd had the willpower and clarity to walk away from the drugs and alcohol and gotten a good night's rest. He might have been better prepared for what had happened on that wave; but one ill-advised night of fulfilling his animalistic desires had changed the direction of his life, and he'd have to live with that truth.

Jaime spent the following weeks in the surf shack behind his parents' house, leg in the air, on the roller coaster of pain-killers and dull sleep, smoking pot at all hours and watching television to pass the time. He had been given exercises by a physical therapist that he could do while in bed, as well as herbal balms and ointments to speed the recovery process and lessen the pain. It wore on him every day, knowing that he had to wake up and do these mundane exercises to get his mobility back. Instead, he chose to get high; he doubled his dosage of pain pills and viewed meaningless sitcoms and played video games to distract himself from what he needed to do. If he had worked diligently on his rehabilitation, his injury would have become a lesson, an opportunity to see that our choices create the fabric of our lives. But he couldn't get a clear picture of his recovery, and he knew no one who'd been through something like this and might have set him straight. So he allowed visions of defeat and self-loathing to take over his thoughts, and withdrew into himself to bathe in his identity as a victim of circumstance.

His good friends stopped by to help him out and give him support, as well as whatever drugs he needed. Bullet-Head Point's code of conduct was *live and let live*, for each person was an individual and had the right to live life as they chose, even if it was to their detriment. The medications Jaime was consuming were devouring him from the inside out, as was his diet, which consisted of sugary sodas, takeout pizza, and chemically derived, processed snacks. Slowly he was slipping into the void of "what could have been" and away from "what will be." Friends and family tried to boost his spirits, but he was indifferent and playing the part of Poor Me. He had by now become indifferent to the near-death experience he'd had, including the proclamation issued by the holy being that had sent him back for reasons yet unknown.

His mother tried her hardest to intervene. "Jaime, pull yourself out of this funk. This isn't the end of the world," she said, as he lay like a statue on his bed. "You have your whole life in front of you," she pleaded, but the drugs made him care less about her words.

"When my leg heals I'll get out and about, I promise," he mumbled, anxious to end the daily lecture.

Ivette wasn't happy with his coldness and overuse of drugs and pain-killers, and she was losing faith that he'd bounce back from the accident. As the weeks passed she became increasingly unhappy. She stopped coming by on a daily basis, claiming that she needed space. Jaime didn't show it, but her absence added to his agony in a big way and broke his confident spirit. In his numbed state of mind and physical lethargy, his once lean and muscular frame was reduced to skin and bones. He was becoming a skeleton and could summon no motivation to help himself. Jaime didn't have the wisdom that comes from experience, to see that success is not without its hardships, and that with a shift of perspective and some positive support, he could turn the situation around. This was a test and a lesson, the universe's emergency broadcast system guiding him to wholeness.

Three months passed, ninety gloomy days that never seemed to end, and the first contest of the season was set to begin. His leg had been in traction for a month, and when it came time for him to walk he had to do so with crutches. Putting pressure on his foot sent a lightning bolt of pain to his head, so he opted to stay in bed except for the basic necessities. When the day came for Jaime to either declare his injury or surf his heat, he made the only decision he could, to withdraw. He told himself he'd be able to surf the next contest in a month, though his imaginings were a product of his fading vision of reality. His mother took it upon herself to call the contest director, who said Jaime would be missed on the tour and hoped he would get well soon. When his mom relayed the message to Jaime as he lay comatose in bed, she embedded a pod of hope, even though he did not seem to register her words.

His pain-killers weren't working anymore, although his discomfort was more mental than physical, and he craved something stronger to numb his brain. With his life in disarray, Jaime asked a friend to have Rags get him some heroin. Rags came by in the middle of the night, sneaking over the back fence to deliver what Jaime desired. It was a disastrous choice, but Jaime knew the drug's strength as a pain reliever, and this was justification enough in his twisted state of mind. He had tried it a few times, vomited and passed out, but had also experienced the attractive side of the extremely addictive elixir, how it reduced all problems to inconsequential bubbles of love. But this form of love came with a price: if you walked through that door, Dante's inferno would become real, and you'd be lost in a hellish underworld that you needed the strength of a champion to break out of.

In the privacy of his bathroom, which had only a ceiling fan for exhaust, he'd chase the dragon, as the addicts called it, heating the brown substance with a lighter under tinfoil. For days upon days he fell into an incoherent void. Angels and demons visited him, competing for control of his consciousness, and a million needles of pain pierced his body unless he consumed the smoke of the burning oil. It tasted and smelled like a rubber tire, spread finely over a piece of aluminum foil. At one point, a recognizable figure came into his haunted castle, and said she didn't want to be with him anymore because she couldn't stand to see him in this condition. Jaime laughed at what he believed to be another apparition, failing to grasp that his girlfriend was leaving him for good.

His father also stopped by, drunk as ever, to laugh at his predicament. “I told you, Jaime-boy, all that fame got to your head and look at you now.” His drunken laughter echoed off the walls of the maze Jaime was trapped in. Or maybe it was just his mind playing tricks, as he slid down the water slide of hot tar into oblivion.

Soon he was shown other ways to get his heroin fix, by snorting it or by shooting it into his veins, and if it weren’t for his mother’s watchful eye he most likely wouldn’t have lived. She sometimes stayed up all night, pounding on his door as he dwelled in another dimension in the bathtub or sprawled, lifeless, on the floor. When he was able to walk without crutches and started going out of the house, she’d ask him where he was off to, and try to block him from leaving. He’d make up an excuse of some sort, but she could see the signs of his addiction taking over. He itched his body uncontrollably, and wouldn’t look into her eyes. She had to hide anything of value, including the keys to her car; her son’s sickness knew no bounds, and he’d steal anything to barter for his next fix.

Having lived for years surrounded by addicts and alcoholics, Jaime’s mother knew that all she could do was give love and support to those who had gone over the edge into the realm of darkness; but this was her only son. She tried and said everything in her power to turn his life around. She saved him over and over, even climbed through a window once, when she saw him choking on his vomit in his sleep. After that she demanded a copy of the key to his door. She would shoo away shady-looking characters that approached their property, but Jaime would find ways and people to deliver his poison. He was now utterly addicted to it, and on a course toward complete self-destruction.

At one particularly low point, unable to support his ever-growing heroin habit, he was offered a way to make some quick cash from a local drug dealer. All he had to do was make a few deliveries, and he'd receive as payment his daily fix and more, plus he'd get to drive around in a badass Mustang and have some pocket cash. He no longer thought of surfing, the ocean, his friends and family; all that mattered was his sick craving and desperate need for the drug that was his obsession.

Late one night, Jaime had a product drop-off on a side street in a middle-class neighborhood. He had been here many times; the user was a businessman who supplied his associates with their needs, as well as satisfying his own voracious appetite for the chocolate-colored goo. As Jaime pulled up to the house, the area was unusually quiet, the only sound the wind whistling through the Magnolia trees that lined the sidewalk. He grabbed his camouflage backpack loaded with the goods, and casually walked toward the front door. Off in the distance a dog barked, and others in the vicinity joined in a call of the wild. Without warning, Jaime was thrown to the ground, and guns were drawn all around him. "Freeze, you're under arrest! You have the right to remain silent," said a DEA agent, who proceeded to read him his rights.

Jaime went into shock, a stunned remorse; but worse than that was a sickening fear that he might not get to shoot up for twenty-four hours. He was handcuffed, placed in the back of the police car, and driven downtown to jail. After they took his mug shot, in which, after not even a year of drug abuse, he looked ten years older than he was, he was stripped and searched, a guard unmercifully probing his private parts for his stash. Completely humiliated, he was given a dull orange jumpsuit and thrown into a cold, damp cell with a dozen others.

"No way, is that Jaime-boy? Bullet-Head Point's golden child?!" a wiry inmate squealed, his tone feminine. It was

Tweaky, one of the local druggies, who had been in and out of jail for years. Now a middle-aged man—or woman, as he was known to some—he had adopted the role of prison bitch. Jaime sat with his back against the hard wall. This scene was a direct result of his actions; he had created all of it; but in an addict's fervor, he could only curse the world and think incessantly about his next fix. He knew he had to show strength, or else be taken advantage of by other inmates. He had heard horror stories about unprovoked beat-downs, gang rape and forced sodomy.

Tweaky came and sat by Jaime and asked him what he was in for. Looking at the track marks all over Jaime's wrists, he said that he knew a way he could get high. Jaime knew what he was alluding to, and even though he felt the life-draining tractor beam of heroin pulling at his soul, he wouldn't go so far as to perform a sexual act to break its hold on him. Or would he?

Sweat poured from every gland. Just when he felt he couldn't take any more pain, a guard came to the door and called his name. Apparently he was being released on a technicality: the product in his backpack had turned out to be blocks of compressed sand, not heroin. Had his dealer known, or was he being set up? This he'd never know. He was a pawn of the game, and would return to the streets, and his spot on the chessboard of life.

As the weeks turned into months, there was only one fixation in Jaime's mind. He spent much of his time with Rags, shooting up in caves along the seashore and in freeway underpasses. It had all started so harmlessly, only wanting relief from the external world, a lifeline to pull him out of his self-created nightmare. But now, cast into the gaping maw of the brown heroin bear, its teeth piercing his veins, he did not know, or even care, how this shift of perspective would come about. He was in the grips of something beyond his control, and as time passed his options narrowed, until there was only one way out. He had to hit rock bottom before—and if—he was to find salvation.

Chapter 6: Hell on Earth

Jaime awoke in a puddle of his own fluids; with vision blurred, all he could detect was distorted objects and the sound of water dripping against a steel drum. He began to realize where he was, beneath a bridge he had been under many times before. In a heroin-induced delirium, somehow he had managed to find his way here again. Rotting trash, human waste, and other city debris were the decorations of this hollow, damp grotto; used needles and condoms littered the floor, and rats the size of cats ruled the piles of leftovers. The sound of cars going over the bridge above him echoed into the darkness, and in some way this comforted Jaime as he lay there, a remnant of who he once was.

Now in the gutter of existence, he had created hell on earth for himself through his ignorant choices. His past life was a fading memory—surfing, Ivette, his friends and family. Jaime felt sicker and more depressed than he'd ever been, and on the verge of suicide, when in a pile of rubbish he saw a surfing magazine. Jaime himself was pictured on the cover, doing a huge aerial up above a wave.

The image, faded and torn, reminded him of where he was, and of the glory that was not too far in the past. With his last bit of strength, he knew that he needed to seek help, or he would die with the ghosts of regret haunting him. He felt ashamed of the way he had treated his mother when she had given him so much, and he knew he had to make amends to many people for things he couldn't even remember. That's how all-consuming heroin and other hard drugs are: they'll make you hurt, push away, and take from the ones who are trying to help and love you the most. Jaime had done all this and more, and he stood up from the hard cement to return to the only place that might give him shelter and a new start.

He had left his parents' house for the streets after his leg had healed; fortunately, the bones had set properly, but he hadn't done the exercises to get back to where he'd been physically before misfortune struck. If he had made his scheduled biweekly appointments for physical therapy, and kept up with his home exercise routine, he might have been completely recovered in three to six months, contrary to what his doctor had said.

His rehabilitation had been set back even more when his addiction became his only fixation, and he had no motivation to do anything besides feed his sickness. He'd even stolen money from his mother's purse, and he'd sold whatever he could to get high, oblivious to the people he was hurting and unaware of the repercussions. His mother would have given anything to help him, and she'd had her hopes dashed countless times since he had started using heroin, as he claimed he would stop, only to take advantage of her in some way again. This was his last chance, and he knew it.

No one had seen Jaime in several months, though there had been exaggerated stories of his condition and feral lifestyle, and the locals of Bullet-Head Point were surprised to see him walking through the neighborhood. "Jaime brother, there you are!" someone yelled from a doorstep. Jaime nodded with a slight smile, trying not to portray how sick and desperate he was. He looked the part of a street dweller: pale-skinned, with welts and dirty unkempt hair, unshaven and wearing ripped clothes that smelled of sewage. Fearful neighbors peered out their windows as he walked up the driveway to his parents' house.

It was unusually quiet, and he shook with nervousness, knowing what he had put his mother through and wondering how he'd be greeted. Fragrances wafted from arrangements of colorful flowers scattered in pots. He tried to compose himself, tucking in his ragged shirt and slicking back his shoulder-length hair before knocking on the front door. He hesitated, his pale and withered hand halfway to its destination. That's when he noticed the note behind some red roses: *So sorry for your loss, he is in a better place now*. "Who's in a better place?" Jaime muttered, but he knew in his heart that it had to be his father.

Jaime's mom opened the door as he stood there in shock. Her eyes brightened, and she hugged him with a mother's love, intensified by months of wondering whether he was alive or dead. They went inside, and she explained what had happened: his father had died in his sleep from alcohol-induced liver failure. Jaime's mother had been with him through the transition. She was at peace with it, and rejoiced that he was now free. She and Jaime held hands, silently remembering the good times and praying for his soul to be at peace in heaven. The guilt of not being there for his mother or seeing his father before he died broke the spell that Jaime was under; the extreme sadness and remorse he felt marked the beginning of his return from suffering.

His mother invited Jaime to move back into his rustic cottage, but laid down strict ground rules: he had to get off drugs and go through counseling. He was very grateful, though he knew there were challenging times to come. Already he was feeling the itchy, all-encompassing call for his addiction. It ignited every cell in his body, physiologically craving its fuel. But with his father passed and not wanting to end up with the same fate, Jaime seized the opportunity to start a new life.

After he'd left the house for the streets, his mother, devastated and at a loss for what to do, had called Vinnie for advice. Vinnie was an old family friend, someone she knew had been down the same road to self-annihilation, but he had reversed course in a drastic way. Now he worked with Jaime's mother to devise a plan for Jaime's recovery. They'd start, they decided, by shutting him into his cottage to detoxify.

Once Jaime agreed, his mother locked him in from the outside. When it was time to eat, she slid food through the mail slot; he was not to be let out, for any reason or in response to any plea, until a week had passed. The windows were barred; they wanted to make sure he couldn't get out, because if he could, he would. Vinnie knew that Jaime would be begging for mercy at some point, as the withdrawals shifted into another gear of misery.

Several days into detoxification and at the height of his despair, Jaime madly yelled for his mother to open the door. He told her he was fine and wanted to take a run on the beach to work out the toxins. She sat on the other side of the door, wanting to help but knowing that letting him out would be a mistake.

"Please, Mom, I gotta get out of this box, please! Mom, please, they're after me!" he pleaded, horrified and in intense pain. Unseen demons bit into his skin, tearing him apart piece by piece.

"Jaime, I love you," said his mother, "but we agreed that I wouldn't open this door."

If Jaime had been in his right mind, he'd have known that she was saving him from the grave; luckily, he was too weak to cause any harm to himself. Most of his time was spent sleeping and living a nightmare of epic proportions, giving new meaning to the name of the surf spot that had begun this journey. After a week, he had gotten through the worst of the withdrawals. Vinnie stopped by with an inspirational book focused on spiritual values that showed a route out of his predicament. He would read the book to Jaime as he rested, and tell him about his own battle with drug addiction, which had nearly engulfed his life.

Vinnie was in his golden years, although not many knew his real age or his struggles with drugs and alcohol. He preferred to keep his past a secret, but he confided in Jaime because he knew Jaime's family well; he had partied with his father when they were younger, before Vinnie became clean and sober. He saw the cycle being repeated of parents passing their addictions on to their children; his own parents and grandparents had been alcoholics, one hundred percent Native American, inheritors of the sickness of the settlers who'd taken their forefathers' land in decades past. With their culture and traditions stripped and most of their tribe placed on reservations, a few families, including Vinnie's, stayed in their homeland, Bullet-Head Point, which his people then called Giizhigong, roughly translated as "Heaven."

Having been born and raised in a dysfunctional and disintegrating way of life, Vinnie became an alcoholic and drug addict in his teens, an extremist with not one but all substances of that era. Surely he was headed in the direction of live fast and die young, until he met a young surfer who showed him a more fulfilling way to live. This man was the first person Vinnie had seen surfing the waves that rolled into the bay. Mesmerized by this God-like man who floated on water, Vinnie approached him when he came in from his surreal session.

At first sight of him on land, walking like a normal man with his long polished piece of driftwood, Vinnie was speechless. But the surfer, with his bright blue eyes, wide smile, and aura of goodness, won him over instantly with his magnetism and down to earth nature. "Hello, friend, do you live around here? I was wondering if it's OK to surf in this area."

"I've never seen anyone ride these waves, but I have heard stories about the men who ride them," Vinnie said.

The surfer introduced himself as George. After shaking hands, Vinnie invited George back to his house for a homemade alcoholic beverage, as it was high noon and the drink was part of his daily routine. George declined, informing Vinnie that he was just passing through on his way south. They walked to George's wood-paneled vehicle, which he called a "woody," and he poured them each a cup of herbal tea. They drank it as he dried off in the hot summer sun. This was a time before wetsuits and leashes; the surfboards were made out of balsa wood and weighed over a hundred pounds.

George shared a bit about his life with Vinnie, how he had been born and raised on an island chain in the Pacific Ocean, a place where another Indigenous people and culture had been decimated by settlers. But instead of wasting away in defeat, these people became warriors, protecting and carrying on their traditions and fighting until justice was served. George had been an outcast among them, his family having moved there as part of a developer's relocation project to inhabit the islands, but his years as a scapegoat for their anger had taught him compassion and tolerance, and to see the good in others.

George had gone on to become a teacher of sorts, in and out of the water. Now, he told Vinnie, he traveled the West Coast, teaching people about safety in the ocean and rescuing those in perilous situations. He had also recently finished writing a book on the universal truths shared by all religions and traditions, and the common themes that bind them together. He handed Vinnie his book, titled *All Paths*

Lead to the Same Summit, and gave him a prolonged hug goodbye.

As George drove away down the dusty coastal road, Vinnie stood there and asked himself the question brought forth by this serendipitous meeting: “What is my soul’s purpose?” It was the most profound and simple inquiry. Vinnie had never really had a meaning and purpose for his life. Now, he scraped his savings together and took a train to a city four hours away. There were no surf shops back then, and it was days before he found, at a flea market, a used surfboard. And in the weeks that followed, after contemplating the many words of wisdom contained in George’s book, and taking up surfing as his new spiritual pursuit, he resolved to leave drugs and alcohol behind him, and start a new life with the sole purpose of helping others who had traversed the same path.

The book that Vinnie was now reading to Jaime was the one George had given him, the one that had changed his life, and it had the same effect on Jaime: it washed away the desire for everything but knowledge of who he really was, and his purpose in this lifetime. This was the positive support and guidance Jaime craved, to hear that obstacles can be overcome, that the cycle of addiction can be broken as we become grateful for our place in this world, and to find purpose and meaning in a place where they once didn't exist. He now had the motivation he needed to get back in shape, and it wasn't long before he was able to walk outside into the fresh air, taste the salty breeze on his lips, and cry to the heavens that he had survived, and would live to see another day. He began to foster hopes of getting back on the GAST tour and blowing up the ratings, and to reconnect with Ivette; he had put her through a lot, and he wanted to show her that he had changed.

But most importantly, with his newfound strength, it was time to surf again. As he started the process of rebuilding his life, surfing would give him something to focus on. It was his main passion, the beacon lighting his road to redemption, and it was calling him back.

Chapter 7: Back to His Roots

Jaime's first surf session in nearly six months was a shocker. With his surfing muscles atrophied and his lung capacity minimal, paddling out and catching a wave was a feat in itself. He had chosen to surf the inside of a river mouth between surfing territories on a small day, and there was a mellow crowd of beginners. After a few waves on a thick, four-finned funboard, meant for weak conditions, he was able to connect waves to the beach. He wore a squid lid to hide his identity, but many recognized him and hooted at the reinvented Jaime. As he ran up the beach after milking a small wave to the sand, he saw Ivette watching from the cliff. It was the first time he had seen her since she'd broken up with him. He waved, but instead of waving back, she stood up and walked out of sight. Still, the fact that she had been watching gave him hope, and it fired him up to think that there was a possibility of being with her again.

As he made his way back out to the main peak, a familiar face came pumping down the line, on a collision course toward him. Jaime paddled as hard and fast as he could to get out of the way, for this was the rule: if someone is on a wave, the person paddling out gives him right of way. Jaime rolled off his board as the surfer boosted an aerial over him, and was pitched backward over the falls in his wake. The hold-down was minor compared to the embarrassment: the other surfer turned out to be Nate, still in top form and conditioning, and now he was laughing at Jaime.

"Beat it, you friggin' junkie," Nate yelled, paddling swiftly past him. Instead of forcing a confrontation, Jaime held his tongue and decided to let it go; he was learning that revenge is a bitter ally, one that takes you away from equanimity and keeps the cycle of anger spinning. But he couldn't help catching a wave after Nate, and showering him with spray as he paddled back out, showing him that their rivalry was far from over.

Jaime's surfing rehabilitation regimen involved pool and ocean swimming, jumping rope, and a myriad of other exercises for cardiovascular training. He also watched videos of himself and other top surfers riding waves, as a visual aid to identify and correct flaws in his style. He ran on the beach and swam a little farther out to sea each day, with the goal of making it to the one-mile buoy and back.

One day, while watching footage of a recent surfing contest with Sage, Jaime mentioned seeing Ivette at the beach. Sage unconsciously blurted, "It just isn't right."

"What's not right?" Jaime asked.

Sage stared at him with a furrowed brow. "I thought you knew."

"Knew what," Jaime pressed him.

"Oh, man . . . I didn't want to be the one to tell you, but I'm pretty sure Nate and Ivette are seeing each other." This was the soft version of the story; everybody in town knew they were a couple.

Jaime felt like he'd been slapped across the face. He recalled the moment, a few weeks ago, when he had seen Ivette on the cliff. He hadn't realized then that she was there to watch Nate, and he'd never have thought they were dating. For the rest of that day, he couldn't get the thought of Nate and Ivette together out of his mind. He didn't want to believe it was true. It wasn't uncommon in the surfing subculture to travel on the dating merry-go-round, inadvertently going out with the ex of someone you knew, but it never felt good when your turn ended and you had to exit, while another took your place and kept on riding.

He finally sucked in his pride and called Ivette, but she didn't answer the phone. He had read an inspirational quote to the effect that if you really love someone, you have to let her go, and be happy for whatever path she takes. Focusing on that made him feel better, and dissolved the disturbing emotions that were plaguing him. Still, he wanted to see her. In the least, he wanted to apologize; she had stayed with him until the bitter end, when he was at the height of his madness and knew not what he was pushing away. But in his heart, he hoped to win her back.

The next day, he went to visit her, but she had moved out of her cottage and left no forwarding address. Even her landlady in the main house had no idea where she was, or was quite possibly keeping it a secret; she spoke to him in hurried tones through a crack in her still-chained front door. "She's gone I told ya, now leave me alone."

That night, he called Robbie, Sage, and some of the Bullet-Heads to see if they would join him on a scouting mission to find her, so that he could discover the truth and speak his piece. He was still learning to take a step back before proceeding into a volatile situation with turbulent emotions.

The night Jaime, in his drugged stupor, had laughed at Ivette, she'd left him there. She couldn't take it anymore and had no alternative; she had tried everything. She decided to let him find his own way. She had to take care of herself, although leaving him was the hardest decision of her life. As she sped away from his house she called some girlfriends, and they met at the local bar: the Cattle-Whip, where everyone went and mingled. Regardless of where you were from, it was a safe zone to have a good time. That is, until late at night, when many drinks had been consumed and logical thinking became an afterthought.

While her girlfriends were consoling her at the bar, Nate and his crew of Northsiders arrived, most wearing clean white T-shirts tucked into jeans, and caps and beanies emblazoned with the NS insignia. Ivette had always thought Nate was attractive, with his chiseled features and buffed physique, but being Jaime's girl, and a local from Bullet-Head Point, she'd never revealed this to anyone.

Nate walked up and said, in a mocking tone, "Hey, Ivette, where's that loser boyfriend of yours, passed out in a ditch somewhere?" He and the Northies giggled like schoolgirls, and high-fived at the rude remark.

"Hmm, you and your primate make a great couple," said Ivette. Nate laughed wholeheartedly, as he enjoyed a good put-down. But his confidant, nicknamed Gorilla-boy, wasn't as amused. It was a tradition and rite of passage for all surfers to receive a nickname. It was generally the cruelest label possible, evoking the part of yourself that you loathed the most, that became your alias for life—the boys would make sure of that. Gorilla-boy was six feet five, hairier than Chewbacca, and had an affinity for eating bananas. Hence the title given; but in his case, he valued the ego-boosting brand.

That night, drinks were had until the two a.m. closing time, and after a few seductive, green-light looks from Ivette, Nate offered her a ride home. More than anything, he'd have loved to get back at Jaime for beating him in the last qualifying event, even though they had a near-even head-to-head record from their competitive careers. What better way to salt him out than by winning over the smoking-hot Ivette?

It was in the car that she, drunk as she had ever been, confessed that she and Jaime were over, and that she had always had a crush on him. Nate took advantage of the situation and parked on the cliff overlooking his home break. The ocean swells pounded into the rocks, pushing in and out the change of the tides.

"Nate, no, I shouldn't." She halted his advance as he slid his hand under her dress, and up her thigh. But she really didn't want him to stop, and he didn't.

Jaime had no idea of Nate and Ivette's intimate encounter that night, or of the depth of their relationship; nobody wanted to give him the full details for fear that they would send him into a relapse, so all he'd heard was that they were possibly dating. Jaime hoped this was small-town gossip, and he wasn't going to stop until he knew the truth. He figured he might find her at the Cattle-Whip.

As he, Robbie, Sage, and the Bullet-Heads pulled up outside the Whip, they saw that a big pack of Nate's gang was there. Limo-tinted SUVs and big four-by-four trucks were double-parked out front, and loud shouts came from the upstairs lounge. A dozen strong, Jaime and his crew entered and walked the spiraling staircase to the second floor, where most everyone was hanging out and playing pool. All the Bullet-Heads had on their ribbed black tank tops, which highlighted the multitude of colorful tattoos on every body part. Lizard-man, so named for his bald head and lipless mouth, had the most. He had inked small scales up his neck and cut a menacing figure, his biceps as big as watermelons, his pale skin and light-blue eyes making him look like a six-foot salamander. The boys from both sides of town knew and had respect for each other, and they greeted one another amicably, with handshakes and passive-aggressive power hugs. But there was an undercurrent of tension, as time slowed down and all witnessed what was unfolding.

In the shadows of the room, illuminated by a red light, Ivette sat on Nate's lap. Jaime's heart skipped a beat; he felt like he had been punched in the stomach. It was true: she was with him. The discovery threw Jaime into a blind rage. His animal instincts took over, washing away his otherwise calm demeanor and nonviolent stance. He walked over to them, flanked by his Bullet-Head brethren, and asked Ivette if they could talk; he spoke with composure, even though his heart was beating out of his chest. She looked over at Nate, and he replied for her. "Get lost, you has-been. She's mine now, and she doesn't want anything to do with a scumbag like you."

Jaime walked casually over to the pool table. He grabbed a shiny pool stick and, with the quickness of a ninja, smashed it against the side of Nate's head. With this act chaos broke loose, and a rumble began between the Bullet-Heads and the Northies. Gorilla-boy grabbed Sage, picked him up over his head, and threw him against the wall. The Bullet-Heads had their own version of Gorilla-boy, nicknamed Alligator-man because of his many sharp teeth and elongated head. Al for short, he was a dirty fighter, and he jumped on Gorilla-boy's back and bit into his ear. Nate brushed off the blow to his head and squared off with Jaime, once again competing to see who was best.

Nate wasn't a trained fighter, and Jaime, having learned the basics of jiujitsu from his well-trained entourage, quickly had him in a headlock and gasping for air. This was actually a compassionate act in the fighting realm, to put someone in a headlock, without inflicting bodily damage, until they fell asleep. Police sirens could be heard in the distance as Lizard-man dropped his guard against his opponent, and slithered out of sight. Nate passed out from oxygen deprivation, and Jaime dropped him to the ground and let out a high-pitched whistle above the melee, signaling his crew to retreat.

On the drive home, slumped in the back of the Black Beast, he knew that he had lost Ivette and could never be with her again. She'd moved on. A month into sobriety, with a clear mind and dedication to turning his life around, he needed to take responsibility for what had transpired between them. He had just engaged in a violent act, which went against what he was learning about dealing with his emotions and conflict resolution. But he was doing the best he could given the circumstances, and he wouldn't look back in regret. It was officially over, and it was time for him to move on, too. In order to stay on track, he had to leave the past behind, to separate himself from all detriments to his well-being and happiness.

Jaime had begun to see that everything was for a reason and purpose; it was as if there were a preordained plan. No matter his perspective on the challenges that confronted him, all was happening at the right time, for the right reason for his personal evolution. This had played out through the last several months of his life; it seemed an unlikely script that would have him achieve his dream of surfing professionally only to become addicted to a substance with the life-draining force of a black hole. But he was being chewed up by the forces that be, and regurgitated toward a far brighter future than he could ever conceive of. He knew that he had made some uncharacteristic mistakes, but the scars would never let him forget the suffering he had gone through. The end result of using heroin was rarely a pretty sight, in the least a permanent monkey on your back, forever chattering in your ear its blissful tale; but now he was sure that he had the fortitude to never travel that path again.

Chapter 8: The Comeback

Jaime's blueprint for the future involved taking each day, each moment at a time, and working toward the goal that gave his life meaning and purpose: getting back on the Global Assault Surfing Tour. He'd been frothing on surfing thrice daily and training hard for the day he'd compete again, although what would turn out to be the magnetizing force of his intentions was something very different and much grander than his self-centered motives. He was completely sober, even from the relatively harmless marijuana, but still filled with anger, self-loathing, and other emotions that disrupted his inner peace. He had learned that drugs, no matter how fun or recreational, put a bandage on emotional wounds, but once you got off of them, you'd be able to better deal with challenging thought patterns and life's inevitable pitfalls. The old saying *When ye seek, ye shall find* couldn't have been more true; as Jaime sought goodness and direction, the compassionate universe provided him with an opportunity to evolve to a new level of awareness.

A friend, aptly named Lotus for her mesmerizing beauty, called Jaime one day and invited him to a Hatha yoga class.

Lotus was one of the new breed of women surfers that were pushing the level of competence on waves on par with men. Jaime had never tried yoga; he thought it was just some physical exercises practiced by people wanting to get in shape and hippies tripping on acid. But he figured at least it might lead to hooking up with Lotus. What he didn't know was that yoga was an ancient science and discipline that was seeking him, that had thrown him a desirous bait to set him on a new course toward discovering the union of mind, body, and spirit.

In that first class Jaime struggled with the intense physical postures. He felt inferior to the flexible regulars who flowed with the teacher's verbal queues with ease. It didn't help to be surrounded by gorgeous women in tights, and he found that it was best not to stare at them if he wanted to get something out of the class—and if he wanted to avoid being considered a pervert by the ninety-percent-female entourage. One of the foundational movements, downward-facing dog, made his ankles cramp and his back go into spasms, although the experienced teacher helped students stay within their comfort zone and avoid injury by giving adjustments to correct their body alignment. Being upside-down during inversions let Jaime see the world in a different way, and the continuous flow of movement had him sweating out toxins from every cell in his body. A couple of yoginis behind him laughed uncontrollably when he slipped on his sweat-drenched mat during a balancing pose and ripped his shorts. Not long ago, Jaime would have been embarrassed, but he'd learned that the best thing he could do was laugh at himself and get back up.

The part of the class he really enjoyed, the part he found calming and transcendental, was pranayama, or breathing techniques—especially one, called Breath of Fire, that put him in a relaxed yet focused state of mind. Forcefully pushing air in and out of his lungs initially made him cough and gasp, for his lungs had endured years of inhaling marijuana vapors and were akin to two wheezing raisins. But as he mastered the technique, he found that he could do it for as long as he wanted, and that it doubled his breathing capacity. Afterward he'd feel invigorated, and a deep sense of well-being.

Another pranayama that allowed him to detach from the endless stream of thoughts running through his mind was alternate-nostril breathing. This technique involved closing one nostril while exhaling out the other for ten seconds, breathing in for five, holding the breath for ten with both nostrils closed, then exhaling out the opposite nostril for ten, and repeating the pattern for five to fifteen minutes. This was said to bring equal amounts of oxygen to both sides of the brain for improved function, and the ancient yogis believed that if you could regulate your breath, then you could control your mind. Jaime had found a key to turning off the mental motor; for when we concentrate on the breath and hold it, thoughts disappear, and we arrive in the present moment. When the teacher had the students lie on their backs, place their hands on their bellies and breathe in deeply, all the way up to the shoulders, to feel what it was like to take a full-bodied breath, he discovered that he had been shallow-breathing his entire life until now.

"Breath is the prana that flows through us and animates our lives," the teacher said. She also taught the class that a surefire way to stay anchored in the present moment was to practice conscious-breathing techniques throughout the day. "Not only does this oxygenate the body, but it puts us in a balanced mood and connects us with right here, right now," she offered.

At the end of each class, she led them into a guided meditation. She explained that the physical postures and breath work were mainly to teach concentration, and to prepare the aspirant for the main focus of yoga: the journey within. This inner path is commonly called meditation, which is basically sitting in silence and becoming an observer of your thoughts until they dissolve, and reside in a transcendent state. The formula was intriguing and quite simple, and this resonated in Jaime's heart.

Nevertheless, he found it frightening to witness what was going on inside his mind. He had always lived in external reality; his internal world was comparable to an insane asylum, awash with innumerable voices and characters of varied temperaments. He'd grown used to tuning the voices out through entertainment, loud music, drugs, and pointless gossip, but the meditator's objective was to reside in the place between thoughts. One day he spoke with the teacher after class and explained his dilemma, and she gave him a technique that would help him to sit with these voices and remain unperturbed: he was to imagine that his thoughts were wild horses running through a field. She instructed him to give each a color in accordance with an emotional attachment and acknowledge its presence. In the beginning a rainbow of colorful horses galloped through the field of his consciousness, representing the wide spectrum of his feelings, as he sat in a chair, eyes closed and hands folded in his lap; but instead of fright, he felt that it was a thing of magnificent beauty. And a freedom he had never experienced washed over him when he had the realization that he was not these emotions or voices, but that he witnessed them—that they only existed when he became attached to them. When he let go of the reins of identification that bound them together, the emotions galloped away into nothingness and left him in that sacred silence between thoughts.

Jaime was learning that, by being aware of his thoughts, words, and actions, he could choose to create his life in a way that was positive and beneficial for himself and those around him. He saw that he could be an example for others, a guiding light to sobriety. It was his choice which legacy he would leave, and which reality he would live in: heaven or hell. By grounding himself in the present moment and filling his mind with virtuous thoughts, he kept himself focused and in sight of his goals.

Things were changing slowly but surely. He started each day by reciting positive affirmations, followed by writing down what he wished to achieve. He then read aloud, with conviction, what he'd written. He found that doing this had a profound impact on his daily activities and good fortune. As he became more evolved on the yogic path, and focused his thoughts only on health, equanimity, joy, and loving kindness, he released himself from the chains of self-loathing and regret, and encountered positive people and events—life's way of giving back when one devotes disciplined and determined effort toward goodness. Like a magnet, good vibrations attract good vibrations, and Jaime's personal world was filling with friends and strangers willing to help him in every way. He was attracting beneficial forces from all points of the universe through his unswerving intention to become a better man. He was unlocking doors to a joyous life, walking into a new reality that filled him with hope and gave him a reason to live and to love.

His surfing was also showing the effects of his hard work. He found speed and agility in his new boards, and his performance in the water was awe-inspiring. By fine-tuning his skills not just in the point breaks he'd grown up surfing, but in outer reefs and beach breaks of all sizes and wind ferocities, he'd become capable of surfing any conditions; his days were filled with learning, training, and focusing on his intentions to get back on the Global Assault Surfing Tour.

GAST was no longer a party tour, as it had been many years ago. Today, those who qualified were clean and sober athletes. If you weren't at your best in and out of the water, you'd be one of the unknown many who made a halfhearted effort to qualify for the tour and got no results. Jaime hired Eagle Eye, a legendary surf coach who had trained many world champs, to get him up to date on the ever-changing realities of the sport. Eagle Eye showed him how to pinpoint and maximize his strengths and weaknesses as a competitive surfer.

However, the days that followed weren't without difficulties. The demon of addictive substances tempted him many times, often materializing on his darkest days, when his focus and strength were low. But instead of repelling this fictional entity when, without warning, it appeared in his mind-space, he sat with it, asked it what it wanted to teach him. Over and over he found that the entity didn't exist, that it was only a program running in a loop, and that when he shined the light of awareness on it, it vanished. He had found this tool in one of the many books he'd been reading, and it seemed to work quite well. The practice tightened up his inner machine until it ran as quiet and smooth as a hybrid motor, and turned his mind into an ally instead of a foe.

Months flew by now that he was committed to his daily routine. His past seemed as a dream; nevertheless, it had shaped who he had become.

After nearly a year of sobriety, Jaime felt he was ready to surf competitively. He hadn't relapsed and was living a clean existence on all levels. Many in the surf industry knew of his return to the sport and wanted to give him another chance, and he'd received the injury wild card to an early-season GAST event. Everyone had heard about his near-fatal accident at Nightmares, his recovery from drug addiction, and his father's death, so he had a lot of people rooting for him. People love a good comeback story; Jaime was living it, and was once again at the door to greatness.

The third event of the Global Assault Surfing Tour was held at a warm-water sand point a few hours south of where he lived. This spot was renowned for top-to-bottom, dredging barrels that peeled down a shallow sandbar that had been created by a nearby breakwater. The swell had reached six to eight feet and the event organizers had created a tent city on the dunes, mere meters from the high-tide line. Excited spectators were able to watch the surfers perform their ocean acrobatics, disappearing into waves and flying through the air with relaxed ease, under warm and sunny skies with a light offshore wind.

At the height of his surfing potential and more confident than he'd ever been, Jaime entered the area where athletes, coaches, and industry insiders mingled. His competitors in the trials weren't about to give Jaime any slack for his struggles or the suffering that he had recently endured; but a select few gave him high-fives and nods of recognition. They had their own sad stories. Most everyone on tour had experienced a career-changing injury, lost family or friends, or at some point had a hard time finding a sponsor to finance their travels. They all had their eye on the prize, a triple-digit check and a brand-new SUV, and, most importantly, points to climb the GAST rankings; but they recognized Jaime's talent and determination, and knew he was a force to be reckoned with.

Jaime put on his turbosonic headphones and listened to some pulsating beats, going through his pre-heat exercise routine, undistracted by the photographers snapping his picture and inquisitive onlookers pressed against the barricade, screaming for an autograph. The media had sensationalized his return to the sport; whether good or bad, his name and redemption story were in the spotlight.

The time he had waited for had come, the moment he had visualized in his mind's eye: a reclamation of his life, a chance to prove to himself that he could once again achieve greatness. He grabbed his yellow contestant's jersey, hugged Eagle Eye, and jogged to the beach. Fans ran alongside him, vying for his attention, but Jaime's focus was on the waves, winning this heat, and enjoying the journey, and as he jumped into the ocean, he felt infallible.

His game plan was to catch every wave possible with or without priority, and that's exactly what he did. He out-hustled the other contestants and received the first perfect score of the day, for a lengthy backdoor barrel ride that he exited without claiming it. Leaving all others in his wake, he won his first and every subsequent trials heat by a wide margin. The gallery witnessed his demolition of the other surfers, and let out a thunderous roar whenever he caught a wave or did an extreme maneuver. There was no stopping his rise to the top, and it was looking to be a story for the ages.

He was now in the main event, consisting of the top forty-two surfers. His next heat would have three other top-ten surfers in it, one being Johnny Swish, who had three world titles to his credit. The top two surfers of each heat would progress to the next, but Jaime wasn't looking to finish second.

They waited in the channel until the horn signaling the beginning of their heat let out its baritone whistle. Johnny shared Jaime's aggressive mind-set, and they battled for the first wave. Johnny stood up before Jaime and, bottom-turning in front of him, caused Jaime to go backward over the falls. The crowd collectively moaned and gasped as Jaime gathered his senses and paddled for the next wave. His form was flawless, drawing a perfect line to get a five-second tube ride, then out into the open face of the wave to blast multiple turns, with a reverse aerial to end his attack. Fate seemed to be on his side as he blazed through each heat, dominating international competition and upsetting the best surfers in the world to make it to the finals.

Johnny Swish had also advanced to the finals, along with Latin sensation Hector "The Beast" Montana and Europe's best, Jean Claude "Pinot" Noir. This was the top of the class and Jaime's biggest test. The swell had increased over the day and pink clouds sat lazily on the horizon, their hues magnified by the setting sun. The last heat of the day was looking to be a grand finale.

As the finalists paddled out through the inside breakers, a double overhead close-out set caught them by surprise, snapping Jaime's board in half like a twig. He was tired from surfing multiple heats and the rip current was sucking him out to sea. There was no Jet Ski assistance and Eagle Eye, his coach and caddy, wasn't allowed to enter the ocean; Jaime would have to swim to the beach and retrieve his backup surfboard if he was to continue. He bodysurfed the foamy whitewater to the beach and ran to get his other trusty stick. Johnny and Hector had already ridden waves and five minutes had ticked off the clock by the time he paddled out again.

The same rip that had hindered him now delivered him to the lineup like an escalator, in perfect time for the wave of the day to materialize. Taking off under the lip and standing tall in the greenroom of water hidden from his audience, he rode the tube the entire length of the wave until it spat him out, like a baby being born. Primal screams erupted from within him, in chorus with the cheers of the spectators. He still needed a second score, and the judges were looking for a little variety in his turns and some solid barrel riding. Pinot, so nicknamed because of his fondness for red wine, had uncorked a bottle on his first wave by methodically taking it apart with powerful hacks and gaffs, and he'd gotten a clean tube to maximize his ride.

In the dying minutes of the heat, after all of the finalists had given it their best, Jaime sat in second place with a minute remaining on the clock. On instinct, he paddled up the sand point to where it usually wasn't makeable into the bay, and his hunch paid off, as a set came in from the ideal direction. He knew this was it. On autopilot, he surfed better than he'd ever surfed, and he let everybody know this was his day by his incredible performance. The judges awarded him scores of 10 across the board. The horn sounded. He had done it. He'd earned the wild card to surf in the next contest, thus fulfilling his intention of rejoining the tour.

This time, as Sage and Robbie carried him on their shoulders to receive his first-place check and trophy, he didn't want to run away from the masses of people. He felt a oneness with everyone and everything, and he rejoiced in this epic moment. Rags was beating his drum near the podium looking into the sky, most likely high as a kite and with a mesmerized look on his face. Nate and Ivette were there too; she was pregnant, and Nate had dropped out of the qualifying tour and gotten a nine-to-five job to support his new family, learning all too soon how quickly the pro tour can end. He looked perturbed as Jaime and Ivette shared a moment of recollection of their past love, but Jaime harbored no ill feelings. He had forgiven everyone and everything, and he felt no regret or anger. In fact, he viewed his past challenges and enemies as his greatest teachers.

"Thank you for being there for me, Ivette. I know that I put you through a lot, and I will always wish you the best," said Jaime. He offered his hand to Nate, an act of friendship that Nate accepted; even he seemed affected by Jaime's words and goodwill. It was as if a cloud had lifted, freeing them all from the negativity that had surrounded them.

As Jaime once again stood on the winner's podium, looking out into a crowd of people chanting his name, reveling in his triumph over near-insurmountable odds, an indescribable feeling of happiness filled his heart. Jaime's spirit rose above him like a phoenix, and he knew with all certainty that his suffering had been for a purpose: it had taught him to be grateful for all that he had, to be the best he could be, and to strive for a happy and fulfilled life, while giving this knowledge back to others.

Chapter 9: Giving Back

A few days later, as the sun rose on his home break, Jaime witnessed an irate local surfer screaming at a beginner who had accidentally dropped in on him. Down the street, a group of Bullet-Head boys, still in party mode from the previous night's festivities, swigged from a bottle of vodka and accosted passersby. Watching the locals take turns dunking the unlucky surfer underwater, Jaime had a profound epiphany. After what he had been through, he now had a completely different perspective on his community. He realized that there had been some truth to his deceased father's drunken rants on competitive surfing and the state of their local surfing culture—how one's ego could be overly inflated by delusions of grandeur, and how pride in your community, without compassion and respect for others, could become a recipe for anger and needless violence.

This had more to do with the family and community environment that each individual was raised in than the roots of the surfing experience, although many clung to their social masks in search of power over others because they felt so hollow inside, and fearful from lack of self-worth. Too often they turned to drugs and attacks on others in a desperate attempt to escape their inner confusion. This in large part was a conditioned response to how they were treated by their parents and peers in their formative years. Now with a new level of awareness, Jaime saw that the way he felt about others was really the way he felt about himself; and by accepting people as they were, he could better respond to the social challenges that confronted him. Since he had worked on himself in so many ways, he felt he could now branch out to helping others see that what mattered the most was feeling good about yourself. And the way to do this was by becoming more kind and tolerant of others, and by looking at each day and every moment as a cherished gift not to be wasted.

Overflowing with gratefulness to be where he was at, and having satisfied his immediate goals, Jaime felt that his purpose in this lifetime was to help others. People were free to live their lives the way that they wanted. He had no right to judge another's path, but he wanted to be of service to those who desired a new way of living. He would draw from his own experiences to become a beacon of positive change for his local surfing community, and to help others to live a drug free, prosperous and contended life.

It was one of those moments of divine guidance. Some would call it our original life agreement, broadcast back to us in a circle of remembrance. Jaime had received a six-figure purse for winning the contest, and he wanted to do something meaningful with it, something that would change the lives of those who had lost their way as he had. He also wanted to pay back his mother for all that he'd taken during his binge, and offer her something more than money as a way to thank her for her love and care. If it weren't for her giving him another chance, he most likely would be still high on heroin, in jail, or dead.

Jaime discerned that what was lacking in the surfing community was a place for people to hang out in a communal setting without drugs or alcohol, a forum for everyone to discuss life issues in a calm and constructive environment, no matter their race, class, creed, or religious affiliation. He decided to use his contest earnings to create a nonprofit foundation to pull in those lost at sea and bring everyone together for positive change. He would also create a surf-riders club, to steer this ship on its mission to help countless others—a place where everyone could relax and have fun, like a big, extended family, as long as they abided by the rules.

As part of the club's code of conduct, members would be required to leave all negativity outside the premises. Forms of negativity included judgment, violence, and discrimination, some of the main poisons being injected into the community. Jaime's idea went against the ego based mentality of seeing beginning or untalented surfers as kooks, and outsiders as a plague invading their homeland. Of course, the politics of surfing territories was a loaded issue, but Jaime surmised that people could coexist while protecting and regulating their home breaks in a nonviolent way.

The surf-riders club would incorporate all of these values, as well as offer classes for a variety of life skills such as job placement, how to prepare and eat a balanced diet of whole foods, and esoteric subject matter. Members would be able to attend workshops on how to be a better person and live a more fulfilling life, based on teachings without any dogma or religious affiliation. For instance, a lecture on how to be our best, delivered by a surfing legend who had become coach to the world's best competitive surfers, could emphasize saying positive things about others and celebrating their successes in life. The foundation of this teaching was that we are all interconnected, and that by helping others and sharing in their joys and triumphs, you will find the same laid out for you, like a saint's footprints on the path to enlightenment.

After brainstorming with friends and influential surfing figures, including Vinnie, Jaime realized that what most wave riders loved, and had in common, was the camaraderie of the pack. Surfers of all ages liked getting together to watch surf flicks with good soundtracks, or playing games like pool, ping-pong, cards, and other friendly competitions to keep things lively. The center would include a movie room showing the recent local surf footage and surf movies, as well as educational documentaries and other entertaining films, and it would host a Friday night community potluck with an open mike for all to speak their piece. This would give people the opportunity to be heard by their peers and elders, a chance to open their hearts and get feedback from others. Attendees would be asked to bring some form of food and beverage; sharing meals made everyone feel accepted and loved, something that had been long forgotten in the area and in most families. Volunteering and community services would be introduced, such as free counseling, dental and health care, and bags of fresh, whole foods delivered to those in need. In addition, the center would sponsor activities like picking up trash on the beach, checking ocean water quality, and feeding the elderly and homeless. Giving back would be the theme and guiding purpose for the foundation's vision.

There was a lot of work to do, but Jaime knew they could transform their dysfunctional, drug-infested community into a safe and healthy environment. His father's words rang in his ears, all of the drunken verbal attacks decoded to reveal a way to return his community to a simpler, happier time, in tune with nature and community. Jaime understood that, like himself, many youths came from troubled homes, and faced emotional challenges that could stunt their growth and lead to bad choices on their path of evolution. He knew from experience that what these youths needed was unconditional acceptance, support, and understanding—someone to listen without judgment or criticism, but who would also call them on their delusions and give sound advice without falling back on physical abuse or egotism. Jaime knew the perfect person to fill this role.

When he asked his mother, she readily accepted a position as the center's first youth counselor. Together, they would create a new community environment, where youths were nurtured to become the best they could be and given proper guidelines toward personal and collective fulfillment. These family values had never been in place in the history of Bullet-Head Point, where verbal and physical lashings and the beat-you-down-to-size mind-set predominated.

They held the first meeting a month later, after securing a lease on a dilapidated building that had until recently been home to homeless and junkies. Jaime and other locals had remodeled the space, painting it with colorful murals and planting edible plants, a community garden, and a variety of fruit trees, symbols of new life and the limitless bounty of the universe. Families and friends Jaime hadn't seen in ages showed up. He was surprised at how many of the Bullet-Head boys attended. Many gave him power hugs as he greeted them at the front door, some shedding silent tears of hope that they might change their own lives. Even Rags showed up. He didn't want to come inside, but asked Jaime if he could have a few words in private.

"I'd like to . . . do what you did, Jaime—be free from this poison I feed myself every day," Rags confessed. He sounded drained of energy, and had to catch his breath after every few words.

"Come inside and join the festivities, and we can talk more," Jaime responded, putting a hand on his shoulder.

"I can't, Jaime, I have to go find my next fix. . . . But those were the good days, man," he mumbled, losing track of what they were talking about.

"I understand, brother, but tattoo on your mind that we're here for you when you're ready."

Rags forced a crooked smile. He looked back at Jaime as he walked away. Jaime wondered if Rags would survive and return, and with this thought, a new intention was born.

The room was overflowing. People filled the chairs and stood shoulder-to-shoulder against the walls, enjoying each other's company while they waited for the inaugural speech to begin. Jaime had a fear of public speaking, the result of being judged so harshly growing up, and feeling that he'd be ridiculed for his efforts to speak from his heart. As he looked out over the crowd, the scene had a dreamlike quality; you could hear a pin drop as everyone waited to hear what he had to say. He closed his eyes, took a deep breath, and opened himself to guidance. He had learned this surrender to a higher power through meditation, for as we become analysts of the mind and gatekeepers to the thoughts that arrive at the portal of manifestation, we become masters of which words enter and which are turned away.

His speech, which he had practiced numerous times, had some weeping. It struck a chord that rang true with all present, resulting in a standing ovation. He finished by addressing his mother. He professed his love for her, and thanked her for being the one who had opened his eyes to a new world. Seated in the front row, she beamed proudly, simultaneously crying and smiling; and his childhood brothers whistled and started chanting his name.

Sage and Robbie had also turned clean and sober, and had, in addition to the surf-riders club, joined a Buddhist organization composed of misfit youths and unique characters like themselves. They had agreed to have each other's backs for life, and they wanted to help Jaime's foundation in any way they could. "One of the first ways is to stay drug free," said Jaime, "for you guys cannot help others if you can't help yourselves."

They were both skilled carpenters, and they offered their services for the remodel. They also set out to spread the word about the club around Bullet-Head Point. This collaboration took their bond of friendship to new heights, as they worked toward a clear vision of what needed to be done to change themselves and the area they'd grown up in.

Jaime had modeled the foundation in part after another country's program to guide youth in a healthy direction. And as his surf-riders club thrived in the years that followed, it became a model for other beach communities that were inclined to guide future generations in a proactive way. Jaime himself became an ambassador of this movement. People wrote him from all over the country after his foundation was highlighted on a national television network. Other families saw the need for direction in their communities, and franchises with Jaime's framework opened in all the major coastal cities, although any city or municipality inland could substitute its youth's favorite sports or activities for surfing.

With one simple but extraordinary act of giving, by starting his foundation for the "soul" purpose of benefiting his fellow man, Jaime had created a wave of energy and movement that in time changed thousands of people's lives for the better. His dream of qualifying for GAST had actually been an illusion based on the desire for fame and recognition, though this illusion had become a vehicle for transformation. On the familiar bench overlooking the bay, in the spot where he'd sat innumerable times, Jaime carved his father's name into the wood, as a reminder to himself and others of how transitory life is. When his last breath exited this body, he wanted to look back and feel that he had loved life and lived each day to its fullest. Now, being of service to others was his daily fulfillment, and there was no trophy, amount of money, or wave that could make him feel better than putting a smile on another's face and helping them toward a brighter future.

Chapter 10: The Final Mission

Jaime rode his salt-water-encrusted beach cruiser down the winding road that ran along the cliffs. His front wheel squeaked a familiar song that assured anyone within a hundred yards of his presence, but his cushiony seat and oversized handlebars with soft grips made the ride enjoyable. The night was chilly from the fog blanketing the bay; he wore a hooded down jacket, cotton sweatpants, and lambskin boots, his chosen apparel for these ever-changing weather conditions. Just on the outskirts of town, there was a damp cave where the ocean met the beach in a soft embrace. Deep within this cave was Rags, using heroin, slipping in and out of reality and, in his delirium, praying to someone, anyone, for salvation as the walls closed in. This call for help had been transmitted to Jaime from an ethereal source. Some would say it was a higher power, guiding him to help his brother in need, as the cosmic plan unfolded in all its infinite wisdom and majesty.

Rags had once been on the threshold of fame, having graced the covers of surfing magazines before he was eighteen and invented a new aerial maneuver known as the circus flip. He'd had every opportunity to make his mark as one of the most progressive surfers of his time. But for the same reasons as so many others, he had entered the one-way street of heroin addiction. Popular, seemingly cool peers had introduced him to it, and the blissful feeling it gave him had him hooked in an instant. But no one had prepared him for the consequences. Rags hadn't had the proper upbringing or role models, the family or community support to stay away from this ruinous substance. He hadn't been educated as a child about the consequences of doing drugs; he'd been allowed to run free with the pack, and explore the world without parental or societal constraints. He had tried to get off heroin many times since he began, but couldn't seem to stay clean. His behavior had caused almost all of his family and friends to avoid him, and he'd sold or lost everything that was once his as he wandered the streets, begging and stealing for his next fix.

Jaime had lived this nightmarish way of life, and tonight he felt a strong calling to go to Rags. He had seen Rags in a dream, with a bright white light behind him. As the vision drew closer, Jaime had looked into the eyes of Rags, and the eyes spoke an urgent request. Jaime had awoken in a hot sweat, and with a certainty that wasn't his own, he'd gathered his things and set off on the most heroic mission of his life. He reasoned that all you could do for an addict was give them unconditional love and guidance, and you could only help from a distance; once they are too far gone, nobody can pull them back but themselves. One can only be a beacon in the dark night of the soul. Still, he was going to go beyond his rational mind and make a valiant effort to help his friend.

Jaime stashed his cruiser in the bushes above the heroin den. He carefully climbed down the cliff and made his way over a sparkling sand path through the giant boulders, to the entrance of the cave where Rags dwelled. Barely discernible was a dim light, possibly a candle set back in the shadows, and the familiar odor of the burning, brown poison.

He had brought a backpack of gifts for his friend, including sacred crystals that attracted positive energies to one's surroundings and a book on affirmations and prayer—things Jaime had used during his recovery. He softly recited one of the affirmations from the book, sitting in the sand at the mouth of the cave, with the faint light of his friend's body in his sight. It had been given to the world by Swami Vivekananda, a spiritual mystic of the highest order, as a means to help awaken the souls of those who are suffering: *There is no sin in thee, there is no misery in thee, thou art the reservoir of omnipotent power; arise, awake, and manifest the divinity within.*

Jaime left the backpack in front of the cave, with a photo of him and Rags together as kids at the beach, jumping in the air just for the joy of it. He wrote a short note on the back of the picture: *Rags, when you're ready to change your life for good, come over to my house, no one can bring you there but yourself. ~J-boy.*

A few days later, Rags showed up at Jaime's mother's house, where Jaime had been living since his father's death. Rags could barely walk or talk. He looked like a zombie, with pale skin, multicolored bruises and track marks on every vein in sight. Jaime and his mom supported him arm in arm and brought him around back to the surf shack, which was now a recovery cabin for friends who wanted to get off drugs. Jaime's mother had become the official doctor of detox on Bullet-Head Point; this position, and her work with the surf-riders club, had given her a new purpose in life. They had retrofitted the surf shack with foam padding on the walls, and a table for strapping someone down if the withdrawals became too violent. This was the scary face of addiction; the end result of too much pleasure is often unimaginable suffering, as any hard drug user has experienced.

Rags took the train of pain, physically as well as mentally, traveling through the darkest recesses of his soul: to cold, iron-barred prisons of misery with satanic masters who whipped him over and over. He had a recurring dream about a gigantic syringe chasing him, and he ran desperately to escape its reach as it tried to stick him with its silver tip. And it did, and let him know in a shrieking voice that each poke was for every time he had not disposed of a dirty needle properly, and twice as much hot tar was injected in his veins if that needle had hurt a child. His physical symptoms were like he had fallen off a skyscraper and now lay splattered on the pavement, unable to move, fluids leaking from every orifice. As fate would have it, he had a strong enough constitution to make it through the initial two weeks of hell, as his body ridded itself of the toxic substance it had taken in for years.

Following withdrawal, he needed long-term counseling and techniques for living a clean and sober life. Rags trusted Jaime and his mom, and as the days went by they sat together and engaged in conversation about the many things that contribute to optimum health and happiness, the ingredients of a fulfilled life. There was no preaching, only universal truths that he could comprehend and apply to his daily life. The principles of gratefulness, acceptance, and forgiving oneself and others, as taught in many traditions, made Rags feel good and eased years of pain once he began applying them to the skeletons in his closet. Parental issues and abuse from peers disintegrated like a fine dust in the wind of time once he forgave all things, accepting that he couldn't change the past but only learn from it, and be grateful for the chance to start anew.

One book Jaime had given him, *The Yoga Sutras*, laid out a protocol for understanding the mind and achieving mental and emotional harmony. It was basically a map for navigating the river of life, with its many currents and streams, its side canals veering away from, but always flowing into, the infinite ocean of existence. This book gave Rags simple, easy-to-understand teachings and showed him a path to peace of mind. And one affirmation, the one he knew was most important, was branded in his psyche as he walked his new walk, and entertained beneficial thoughts and feelings:

I always have something to give and I give it, whether it be a kind thought, word, or action, and as I give unconditionally, I open the way to receive the endless abundance of the universe.

During one of their private meetings, after Jaime told him about his near-death experience at Nightmares and how it had changed his life in a profound way, Rags confided what he had gone through mentally in those first two weeks of recovery. "You know, I'll admit that I wanted to die, but there was something greater than defeat, something that wanted to live," said Rags. "It revealed itself as the most wondrous and loving presence, and it filled me with complete exaltation when I felt that my life was over. It showed me a vision of who I was to become, and I understood that this wasn't my time."

This withdrawal episode, whether real or imagined in his heroin fever, gave him a new outlook on life and cleaned all unhealthy programs from his mind. As the weeks passed and brain cells slogged off the sticky coating of poppy residue, he became excited about the possibilities that were now arising. He found that there were countless others who had had near-death experiences like Jaime and himself, after which they had undergone the same drastic changes in their perspective on life. Rags knew he had been given another chance, just as he had asked and prayed for, and he resolved to spend the rest of his life giving back to others by whatever means possible, and to live a sober, healthy lifestyle.

He was thrilled to join the local surf-riders club, and he took up surfing again, which filled a place in his heart that had been hollowed by discontent. Once back in the water, he bathed in the surfer's antidote to the chaotic swells of life, and found that Mother Nature had always been there, patiently waiting and ready to soothe his pain. Now she welcomed him back with her liquid embrace. The one thing that had kept him in reality during his druggie days was the drum that he beat at the seashore, and he used it still to return to that place of paradise, but now with a natural high instead of a chemical one. He also started volunteering at Food for Folks, an organization that brought food to the elderly. He'd sit for hours with them, and they happily listened to his babble and offered him gems of guidance drawn from their life stories. But what transformed Rags the most was working in the club's community garden, feeling his hands in the rich earth and the sun on his back, harvesting juicy fruits from the trees, green veggies and aromatic herbs. At these times he understood that surely this was a beautiful life, and each soul, like his, had the capacity for change and growth if given the chance and right setting.

Jaime had accomplished a huge achievement: he had helped someone live a better life. Maybe he hadn't changed the course of the world, but he had affected someone else, one person, in a positive way. He knew that he didn't have all the answers, but if he walked through the world with love and compassion for himself and others in his heart, his mission in this life would be complete.

The ocean mafia, the community that he once felt he had to get away from, had turned out to be the place he needed to stay. Jaime had learned the all-encompassing lesson that we must start with ourselves if we are ever to ignite change in others and our immediate and collective environment. A breath of fresh ocean air had descended upon Bullet-Head Point, and a new era dawned on the community, as they came together to work for the common good.

Jaime sat once again on the cliff overlooking the ocean, but this time with a clear mind as he contemplated the complexities of life and watched surfers compete for waves. Some grommets were learning to surf on the inside breakers, laughing and enjoying life as children do, and

Jaime postulated that educating and communicating with them about life's inescapable challenges would be the biggest factor in their development. In this way, the community would evolve for future generations, and they would be prepared for the lessons to come.

Two playful dolphins jumped high in the air, their synchronized bodies creating a yin and yang symbol. They were far enough away from the children so as to not scare them, yet close enough for them to see, and squeal in delight at the sign they didn't yet comprehend. This was all Jaime needed, an omen of the next adventure in his charmed life.

About the Author

Chris is a fourth-generation Californian who started writing at the young age of fifteen, as creator and co-editor of *Disregarded*, a punk rock fanzine. He went on to write for various websites and magazines on travel, health, spirituality, and extreme sports. He is also a certified yoga therapist and holistic health counselor, as well as an insatiable world traveler. He spends much of his time surfing, writing, exploring nature, and creating art, while studying a myriad of spiritual traditions.

www.ingramcontent.com/pod-product-compliance
Ingram Content Group UK Ltd.
Pitfield, Milton Keynes, MK11 3LW, UK
UKHW041937190726
13854UKWH00004B/1642

9 781304 849588